In Cooperation with the National Park Service

A Servicewide Benthic Mapping Program for National Parks

By Christopher S. Moses, Amar Nayegandhi, Rebecca Beavers, and John Brock

Open File Report 2010–1264

U.S. Department of the Interior
U.S. Geological Survey

U.S. Department of the Interior
KEN SALAZAR, Secretary

U.S. Geological Survey
Marcia K. McNutt, Director

U.S. Geological Survey, Reston, Virginia 2010

For product and ordering information:
World Wide Web: http://www.usgs.gov/pubprod
Telephone: 1-888-ASK-USGS

For more information on the USGS—the Federal source for science about the Earth,
its natural and living resources, natural hazards, and the environment:
World Wide Web: http://www.usgs.gov
Telephone: 1-888-ASK-USGS

Suggested citation:

Moses, C.S., Nayegandhi, Amar, Beavers, Rebecca, and Brock, John, 2010, A Servicewide Benthic

Mapping Program for National Parks: U.S. Geological Survey Open-File Report 2010-1264, 82 p.

Contents

Figures

Tables

Acronyms and Definitions

AGDS – Acoustic Ground Discrimination System

ASIS – Assateague Island National Seashore

ASTER – Advanced Spaceborne Thermal Emission and Reflection Radiometer (NASA satellite)

ATRIS – Along-Track Reef Imaging System: a bottom visualization system developed and deployed by the USGS for benthic mapping and validation.

AUV – Autonomous Underwater Vehicle

AVHRR – Advanced Very High Resolution Radiometer (NOAA satellite)

BCC – Biotic cover component of CMECS Version III

BIO – Bedford Institute of Oceanography (Canada)

BISC – Biscayne National Park (Florida)

BUIS – Buck Island Reef National Monument (U.S. Virgin Islands)

CACO – Cape Cod National Seashore (Massachusetts)

CANA – Canaveral National Seashore (Florida)

CHIS – Channel Islands National Park (California)

CMECS – Coastal and Marine Ecological Classification Standard

DRTO – Dry Tortugas National Park (Florida)

FGDC – Federal Geographic Data Committee

GFC – Geoform Component: one of the three components used to describe bottom habitat in the CMECS (Version III) classification system that focuses on the geologic structure of the bottom.

GIS – Geographic Information System

GLBA – Glacier Bay National Park and Preserve (Alaska)

GOGA – Golden Gate National Recreation Area (California)

GOS – Geospatial One-Stop

GPS – Global Positioning System

GUIS – Gulf Islands National Seashore (Mississippi and Florida)

IKONOS – Not an acronym; commercial high-resolution satellite operated by GeoEye

IMAC – Inventory and Mapping Advisory Committee (NPS)

IMT – Incident Management Teams

IWG-OCM – Interagency Working Group on Ocean and Coastal Mapping

JSOST – Joint Subcommittee on Ocean Science and Technology

KAHO – Kaloko-Honokohau National Historical Park (Hawaii)

LED – Light Emitting Diode

Lidar – Light Detection and Ranging; an instrument that can be mounted to aircraft and uses a laser for determining elevation or bathymetry.

MODIS – Moderate Resolution Imaging Spectrometer (NASA satellite)

MLLW – Mean Lower Low Water

MMU – Minimum Mapping Unit

NASA – National Aeronautics and Space Administration

NOAA – National Oceanic and Atmospheric Administration

NPS – National Park Service

OCRB – NPS Ocean and Coastal Resources Branch (Ft. Collins, Colo.)

PDF – Portable Document Format: easily readable digital-file format for text and figures.

PRF – Pulse Repetition Frequency (lidar)

ROV – Remotely Operated Vehicle

SAV – Submerged aquatic vegetation

SBC – Sub-Benthic Component

SBMP – Servicewide Benthic Mapping Program

SGC – Surface Geology Component

SLBE – Sleeping Bear Dunes National Lakeshore (Michigan)

SST – Sea Surface Temperature

USGS – U.S. Geological Survey

VIIS – Virgin Islands National Park (U.S. Virgin Islands)

WCC – Water Column Component; one of the three components used to describe bottom habitat in the CMECS (Version III) classification system that focuses on the nature of the water column overlying the bottom.

A Servicewide Benthic Mapping Program (SBMP) for National Parks

By Christopher S. Moses,[1] Amar Nayegandhi,[2**] John Brock,[3] and Rebecca Beavers[4]

[1]National Oceanic and Atmospheric Administration, Office of Oceanic and Atmospheric Research, Silver Spring, MD 20910.
[2**]Jacobs Technology Inc., St. Petersburg Coastal and Marine Science Center, St. Petersburg, FL 33701. (** Corresponding Author).
[3]U.S. Geological Survey, Coastal and Marine Geology Program, Reston, VA 20192.
[4]National Park Service, Natural Resources Division, Denver, CO 80225.

Executive Summary

In 2007, the National Park Service (NPS) Inventory and Monitoring Program directed the initiation of a benthic habitat mapping program in ocean and coastal parks in alignment with the NPS Ocean Park Stewardship 2007-2008 Action Plan. With 74 ocean and Great Lakes parks stretching over more than 5,000 miles of coastline across 26 States and territories, this Servicewide Benthic Mapping Program (SBMP) is essential. This program will deliver benthic habitat maps and their associated inventory reports to NPS managers in a consistent, servicewide format to support informed management and protection of 3 million acres of submerged National Park System natural and cultural resources.

The NPS and the U.S. Geological Survey (USGS) convened a workshop June 3-5, 2008, in Lakewood, Colo., to discuss the goals and develop the design of the NPS SBMP with an assembly of experts (Moses and others, 2010) who identified park needs and suggested best practices for inventory and mapping of bathymetry, benthic cover, geology, geomorphology, and some water-column properties. The recommended SBMP protocols include servicewide standards (such as gap analysis, minimum accuracy, final products) as well as standards that can be adapted to fit network and park unit needs (for example, minimum mapping unit, mapping priorities).

- **SBMP Mapping Process.** The SBMP calls for a multi-step mapping process for each park, beginning with a gap assessment and data mining to determine data resources and needs. An interagency announcement of intent to acquire new data will provide opportunities to leverage partnerships. Prior to new data acquisition, all involved parties should be included in a scoping meeting held at network scale. Data collection will be followed by processing and interpretation, and finally expert review and publication. After publication, all digital materials will be archived in a common format.

- **SBMP Classification Scheme.** The SBMP will map using the Coastal and Marine Ecological Classification Standard (CMECS) that is being modified to include all NPS needs, such as lacustrine ecosystems and submerged cultural resources. CMECS Version III (Madden and others, 2010) includes components for water column, biotic cover, surface geology, sub-benthic, and geoform.

- **SBMP Data Archiving.** The SBMP calls for the storage of all raw data and final products in common-use data formats. The concept of "collect once, use often" is essential to efficient use of mapping resources. Data should also be shared with other agencies and the public through various digital clearing houses, such as Geospatial One-Stop (http://gos2.geodata.gov/wps/portal/gos).

To be most useful for managing submerged resources, the SBMP advocates the inventory and mapping of the five components of marine ecosystems: surface geology, biotic cover, geoform, sub-benthic, and water column. A complete benthic inventory of a park would include maps of bathymetry and the five components of CMECS. The completion of mapping for any set of components, such as bathymetry and surface geology, or a particular theme (for example, submerged aquatic vegetation) should also include a printed report.

Introduction and Background

Introduction

Coastal and marine National Park Service (NPS) unit managers and policymakers face an increasing number of complex, interacting factors that impact the natural environment within parks. Some of these stressors include rising sea-surface temperatures (SSTs) (Casey and Cornillon, 2001; Jokiel and Brown, 2004), coastal development (Hooper and others, 2005), erosion, increased nutrient influx (LaPointe, 1997; Hu and others, 2004), overfishing (Davis, 2008), and rising sea level (Done and Jones, 2006). Many of these issues are spatial in nature (for example, marine protected areas in fishery management) and will need new mapping initiatives before monitoring (Anderson and others, 2008). The impacts of natural and anthropogenic processes occur at multiple spatial scales in ocean and coastal environments. Management of submerged resources across spatial scales requires a habitat classification system; application of classification systems requires explicit information about ocean and coastal habitats at multiple scales (Anderson and others, 2008). Numerous schemes have been and are being proposed (Greene and others, 1999).

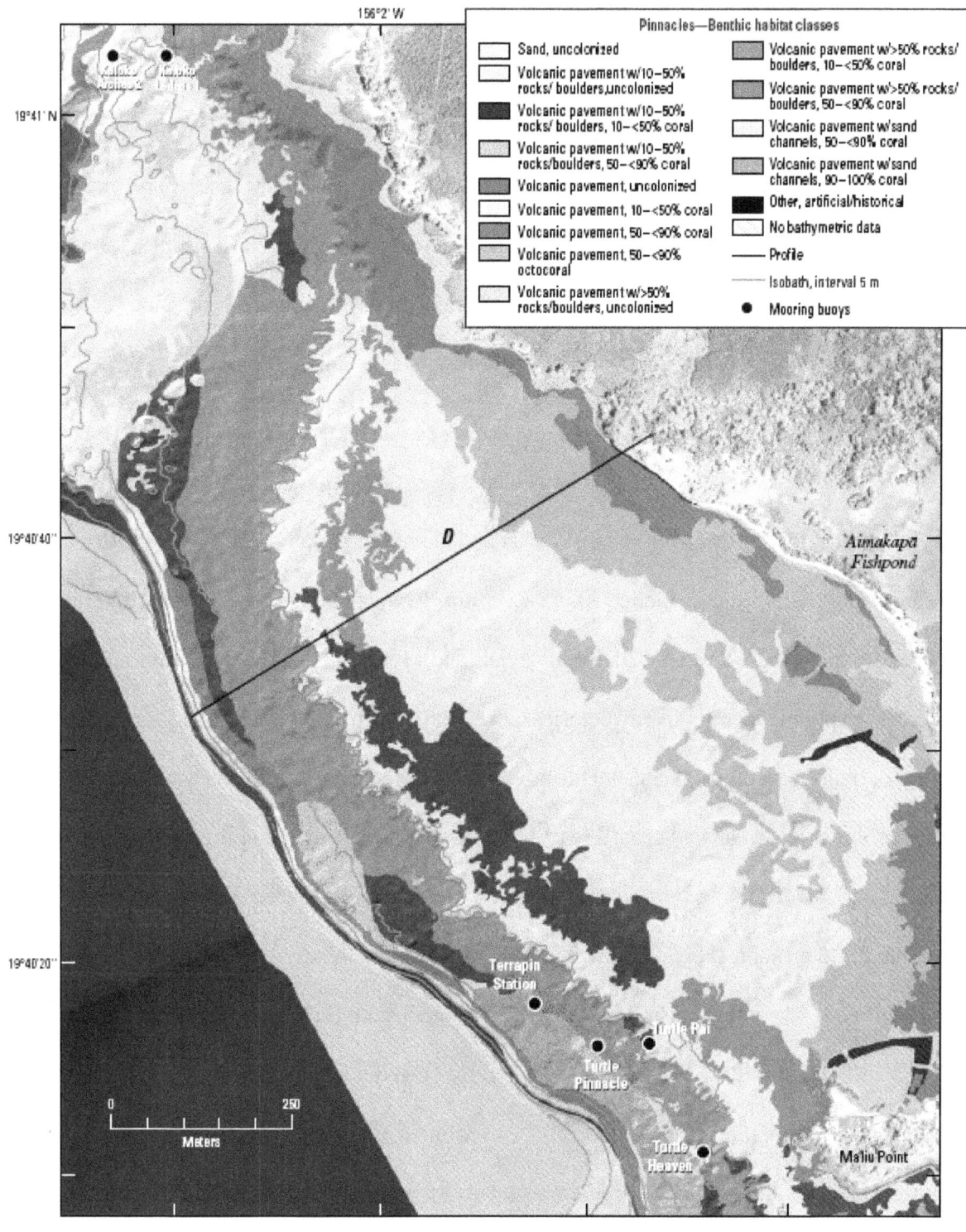

Figure 1. Benthic resource map from Kaloko-Honokohau National Historical Park (KAHO), Hawaii (Gibbs and others, 2007).

The first step to managing for, or mitigating, natural or anthropogenic threats is to know the identity and location of submerged natural and cultural resources in each coastal and Great Lakes park unit (fig. 1). The boundaries and distribution of terrestrial park features, such as forests, roads, vegetation, and soils, can be readily determined. In many cases, park employees can make daily, weekly, or monthly observations of terrestrial features with simple equipment. However, key submerged environmental features are difficult to accurately inventory or assess, often requiring expensive and sophisticated remote-sensing technology, producing results that are subject to multiple interpretations.

NPS officials are developing a Servicewide Benthic Mapping Program to address the lack of benthic inventory information in most ocean and Great Lakes parks. The Natural Resources Inventory and Monitoring Guidelines (NPS 75) (http://www.nature.nps.gov/nps75/nps75.pdf) provide the standards expected for NPS Inventory and Monitoring (I&M) programs and products but do not explicitly identify the inventories. The NPS 77 (http://www.nature.nps.gov/rm77) identifies "marine resource management" as a necessary focus for the NPS. To effectively manage submerged ocean and coastal resources, managers must map and inventory biotic and abiotic components of the environment. The NPS Geological Resource Division's Coastal Mapping Protocol Workshop at Canaveral National Seashore (CANA) in June of 2002 (Nelson and Beavers, 2002) first addressed the need for an organized marine mapping program. In December 2007, the NPS I&M Advisory Committee (IMAC) recognized the need for an ocean and Great Lakes mapping program to support inventories of coastal resources. The IMAC recommended that the NPS I&M program dedicate 5 percent of inventory funds to submerged resource inventories in the ocean and Great Lakes parks (fig. 2). In June 2008, a joint NPS – U.S. Geological Survey (USGS) benthic mapping workshop in Lakewood, Colo., brought

8

together experts to provide recommendations to develop a Servicewide Benthic Mapping

Program (SBMP) (Moses and others, 2010).

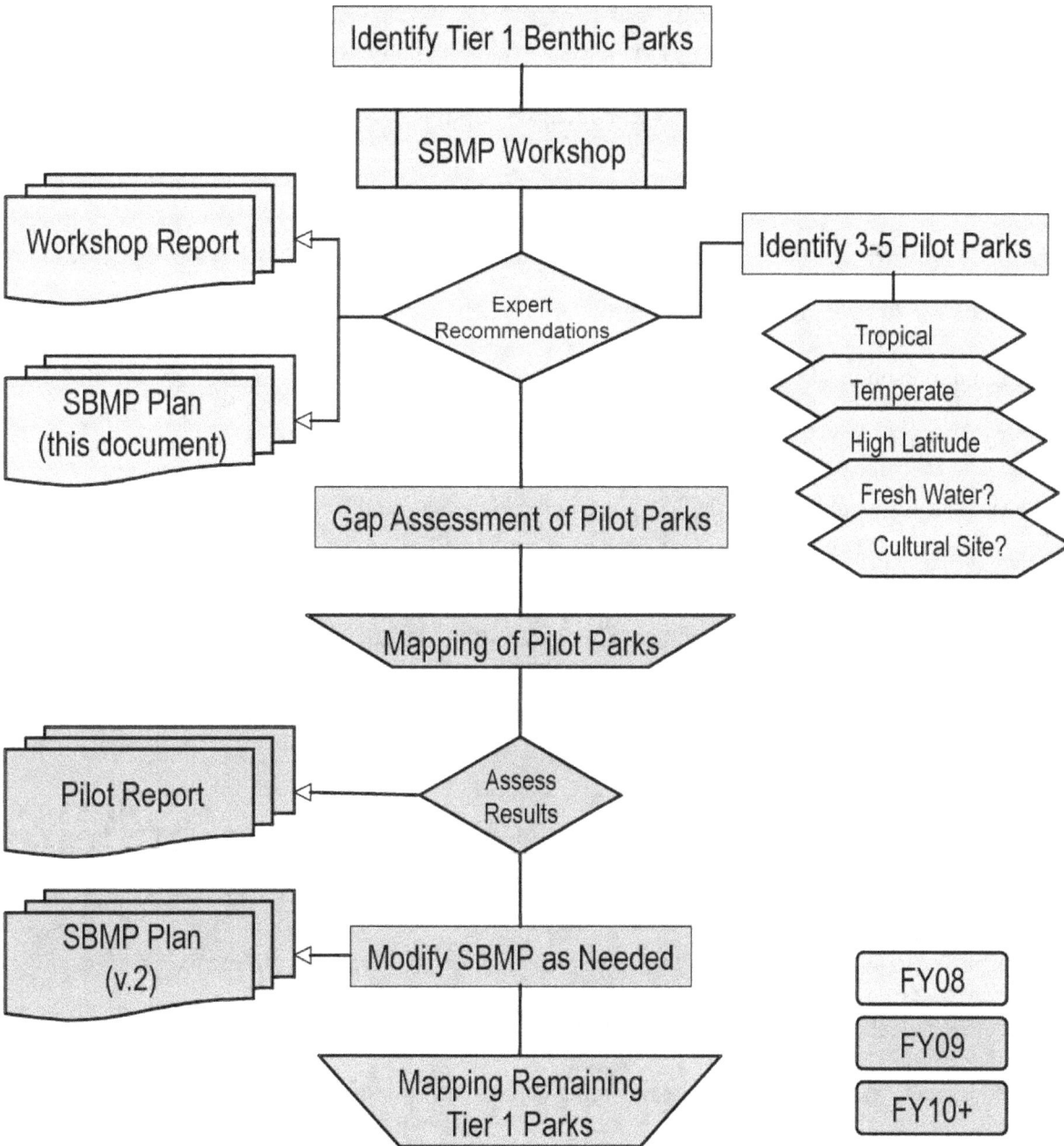

Figure 2. Planned initial phases of the NPS-USGS Servicewide Benthic Mapping Program.

Need for a Specialized Servicewide Benthic Mapping Program

A benthic mapping program is necessary for the management and protection of ocean and Great Lakes parks. The first step is to identify the coastal habitats or environments that are present and then map (i.e., inventory) the classes. With a complete, accurate benthic map, successful management of submerged lands will be possible.

The ocean and coastal inventory and mapping program is distinct from other I&M mapping programs because of the complexities of benthic environments in ocean and Great Lakes parks. These complications fall into two broad categories: (1) technology and (2) commingled resources and features. The technical complications are most strongly manifest in the cost of working in the ocean and coastal environments. The acquisition and processing of acoustic data for a medium-sized park like Golden Gate National Recreation Area (GOGA), with about 15 square kilometers (km^2) of marine waters, or Cape Cod National Seashore (CACO), with 66 km^2 of marine resources, can cost hundreds of thousands of dollars for initial data collection. Validation and interpretation of the collected data add further time and personnel costs.

The issue of commingled resources arises from the coincident nature of inventories in the coastal environment that are easily separated on land (for example, surficial geology and vegetation). An acoustic survey in the marine environment returns a depth measurement and a texture value. Taken together with their derivatives, they could indicate an area of fine mud covered by seagrass. The same acoustic signal carries information for depth and texture. In terrestrial parks, equivalent inventories of topography and soils would be performed in separate surveys. Generally, to define a habitat in the marine environment, the geology, physical oceanography (temperature, salinity, depth, and so on), surface sediments, and biology all need to be known.

Nearshore benthic mapping will inventory vital park unit resources and begin to establish baselines for future monitoring. The benthic maps will identify baseline conditions to inform post-incident (for example, storms, ship groundings, oil spills, and so on) management decisions. With these products, network or regional I&M managers will be able to provide Incident Management Teams (IMTs) with the necessary information to supervise the recovery of benthic resources.

Incidents and sudden environmental changes are not the only reasons for establishing inventories of submerged resources. Coastal regions outside of park boundaries are being heavily developed in many areas, and development is expected to increase over the coming decades. Having accurate inventories up to, and just beyond, park unit boundaries will reinforce any necessary management actions related to development.

Benthic Substrate, Potential Habitat, and Habitat

Historically, scientists and managers have disagreed over finer points of the definition of "habitat." The focus for the disparate definitions revolves around the relative influence of biotic and abiotic factors in describing a habitat (Cogan and Noji, 2007). For this document, and the NPS SBMP, definitions will be applied as follows:

- *Habitat:* a spatially distinct place or environment, defined by biotic and abiotic factors, where an organism or community of organisms naturally lives and grows.

- *Substrate:* the dominantly geological surface on which an organism or community of organisms attaches or grows, such as unconsolidated sediments, boulders, or rock outcrops.

Based on these definitions, most of what is actually mapped by geophysical remote sensing (satellites, aircraft, sonar, and so on) is actually substrate (surficial geology) or *potential habitat* rather than habitat (Greene and others, 2007). For example, multibeam acoustic data may indicate broken columnar basalts on the edge of a large pinnacle. The basalt could be classified as potential habitat for yelloweye rockfish because of their known affinity for those features in some locations. However, whether or not it is occupied by yelloweye rockfish may depend on the season, water temperature, and other factors, such as fishing. Similarly, a satellite image of a coral reef area can be mapped as two classes: sand (high chance of accuracy) and live coral (moderate chance of accuracy because of other organisms that may confuse the sensor and the classifying algorithm). The product is largely a map of potential habitats. The live coral class does describe the habitat of coral-forming organisms but is a poor descriptor since many other habitats (for example, soft coral habitat, hard coral habitat, yellow-tail snapper habitat) are included in the class.

Benthic Mapping Technology

Visible Imagery: Satellites and Airborne

Satellites and aerial imagery are useful for studying a range of ocean and coastal features like SST, bottom structures/potential habitat, and upwelling over scales from 1 square meter (m^2) to 1,000 km^2 or more. Multispectral sensors typically measure the energy in several discrete sections of the visible and infrared spectrum, which is very useful for vegetation and coastal mapping and necessary for SST measurements.

Satellites generally have two kinds of orbits: polar and geosynchronous. Polar orbiting satellites are positioned at altitudes of 700 to 800 km in low-Earth orbit and have orbital inclinations near 90°. The altitude of the orbit dictates the velocity of the satellite, and most polar orbiting satellites circle the globe ~14 times per day (Brown and others, 2005). Depending on the "footprint" (that is, the square area of each image acquired) of the satellite, this number of orbits can result in passes over the same point on the surface of the planet from several times per day to only once every 2 weeks or so.

In contrast to polar orbiting satellites, geosynchronous (also known as geostationary) satellites are in an orbit along the Earth's equatorial plane. To maintain a constant position relative to a point on the surface of the Earth, their orbits are at altitudes of 35,800 km (Brown and others, 2005). Although the resolution of images from geosynchronous satellites, such as weather satellites, is not particularly high (typically >1 km) due to their altitude, those satellites have the advantage of high-frequency, repetitive imagery of the same location.

Moderate-resolution multispectral sensors (that is, sensors that detect electromagnetic radiation in 3 to 30 relatively broad bands), like the National Aeronautics and Space Administration (NASA) Moderate Resolution Imaging Spectrometer (MODIS) and the National Oceanic and Atmospheric Administration (NOAA) Advanced Very High Resolution Radiometer (AVHRR) satellites, provide SST, ocean color, and information on bottom features with a spatial resolution of 250 m^2 - 1 km^2. Higher resolution multispectral sensors, such as Landsat (30-m spatial resolution) and IKONOS (4-m spatial resolution; fig. 3), can be used to map submerged resources in shallow (generally <20 m), clear waters (Andréfouët and others, 2005).

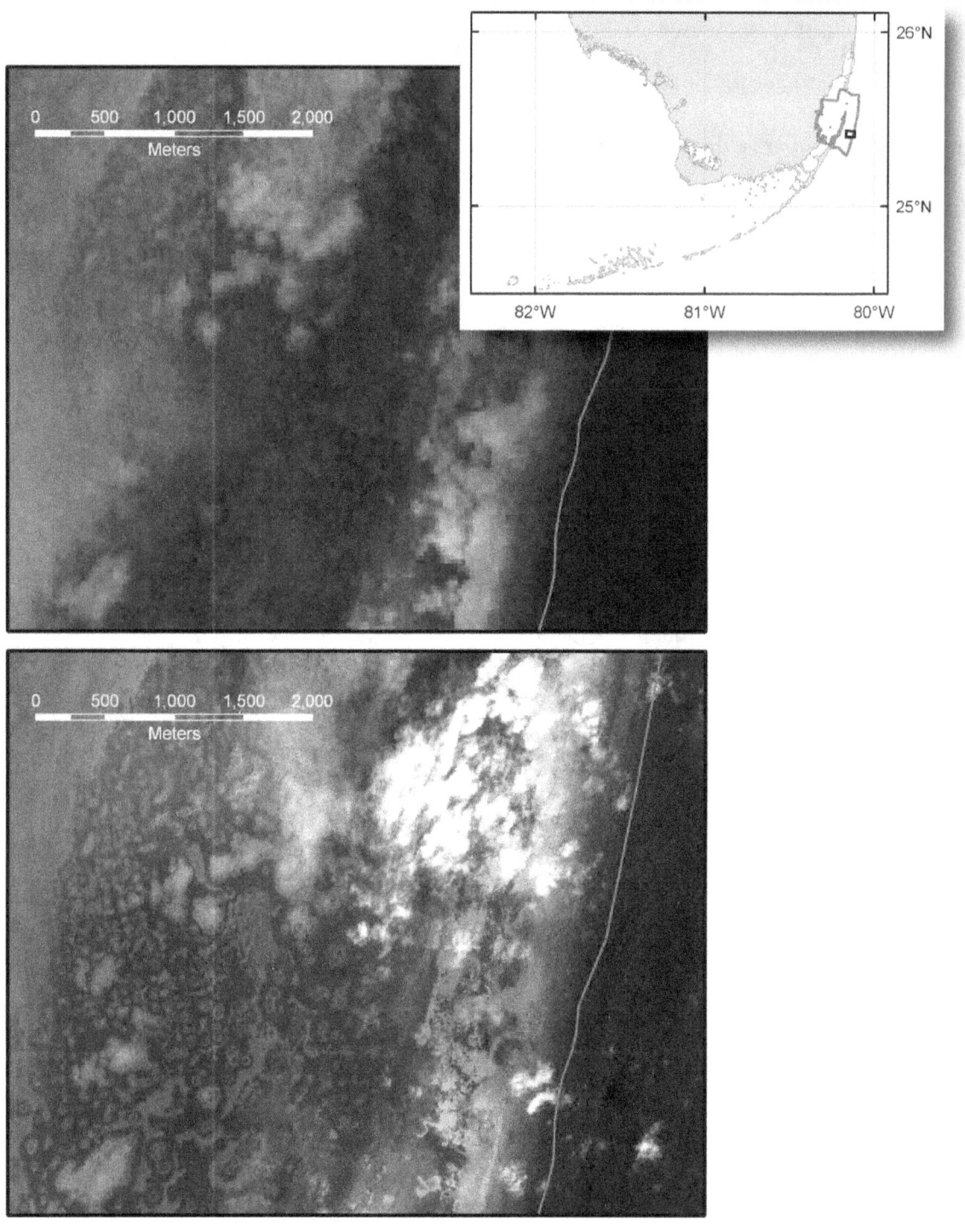

Figure 3. Effects of sensor spatial resolution on benthic mapping in Biscayne National Park. Top frame is Landsat 7 ETM+ with 30-m spatial resolution. Bottom frame is IKONOS with 4-m spatial resolution.

Not all high-resolution sensors are optimally designed for use in coastal environments. NASA's Advanced Spaceborne Thermal Emission and Reflection Radiometer (ASTER) lacks the ability to measure the blue band (450-520 nanometers), rendering it useful in only the shallowest, clearest waters (Brock and others, 2006b). The absence of a blue band on ASTER prevents acquisition of true color imagery of shore-based features as well.

Airborne sensors operate in much the same way as the satellite sensors but can generally provide resolution measured in centimeters because of the much shorter distance to the target. Some of the same limitations apply to these sensors as to the satellites: they work best in shallow, clear water. However, airborne sensors have several inherent advantages over satellite sensors with the same spectral capabilities. The most critical advantage is that the user can define the deployment time and placement of the sensor, which provides enhanced control of the potential for successful acquisition of the target (Myers and Miller, 2005). In many areas or projects, airborne imagery is the only means for success, especially in places with infrequent good weather, or for rare periodic events. In some places, such as the Pacific Northwest, airborne remote sensing is the only way to acquire imagery in the predominantly cloudy environment with wide tidal ranges (Myers and Miller, 2005). In the case of ephemeral events, such as harmful algal blooms, river plumes, or Mean Lower Low Water (MLLW) exposure of benthic features, the flexibility of deployment can make airborne remote sensing the platform of choice if weather prohibits the use of satellite imagery or very high resolution is necessary.

Satellite remote sensing and airborne sensors can also be used to map bathymetry under certain circumstances. Airborne hyperspectral visible and infrared imagery has been used to map bathymetry to depths of 10-15 m in relatively clear waters in the Gulf of Mexico (McIntyre and others, 2006). In tests on Pacific atolls, processing of IKONOS imagery accurately mapped bathymetry to depths of nearly 20 m, but the small rugosity features were accurately resolved only in the shallower waters (Stumpf and others, 2003).

Satellite and airborne remote sensing have been used in several benthic mapping projects in NPS park units, including Biscayne National Park (BISC), Dry Tortugas National Park (DRTO), and Virgin Islands National Park (VIIS).

Multibeam and Swath Sonar

Multibeam and swath (also known as interferometric) sonar use sound produced and recorded through an array of hull-mounted transducers to produce high-resolution, three-dimensional images of the ocean floor (figs. 4 and 5). Multibeam sonar systems can be particularly useful in deep water because of the wide swath covered by the system; however, the resolution is less than in shallow water. The swath of the beam is proportional to the water depth and can range from 1:1 to 12:1 (swath:depth) depending on the instrument and configuration. This means that more passes are needed to map shallower areas, thus decreasing the efficiency of the technique and increasing the acquisition cost per unit area.

Multibeam and swath sonar provide depth to the bottom and information about surficial bottom properties such as hardness and texture (Hughes Clarke and others, 1996; Gostnell and Yoos, 2007). Because these systems are hull-mounted, high-precision corrections must be applied to account for the motion of the vessel, such as pitch, yaw, and roll. These corrections are part of post-processing and can be a substantial portion of the total operational cost in both time and money.

Swath sonar is a particularly useful tool in dynamic environments that can be dangerous to the survey ship. Swath sonar is able to stand off from targets at a distance of ~20 m (horizontal) and acquire reliable data up to 2-m depth (Gostnell and Yoos, 2007). This is important in areas like coastal waters of Alaska, where very steep slopes from shore and offshore pinnacles make navigation for acoustic mapping challenging and dangerous. Swath sonar also increases the margin of safety when mapping in uncharted or poorly charted waters with imprecisely known bottom features that may reach near the surface.

Swath sonar also has an advantage over multibeam systems, permitting broader survey line spacing in shallow nearshore waters because of its greater ability to resolve features across a wider survey track. This reduces both the time and cost required for nearshore surveys. In one comparison test in ~2 m of water depth, a multibeam system required survey line spacing of 7 m, while the swath system acquired similar data coverage with a line spacing of 20 to 30 m (Gostnell and Yoos, 2007). This advantage would provide a time cost of only 25 to 33 percent of that required for multibeam, as well as enhanced safety for navigation of the survey vessel.

The USGS Coastal and Marine Geology Program in St. Petersburg, Fla., and Woods Hole, Mass., uses a SEA Submetrix SWATHplus (2000 series) swath bathymetric system. It operates at a frequency of 468 kilohertz (kHz), and swath width is generally five to seven times water depth. One of these systems was used in 2008-2009 to map the seafloor at Gulf Islands National Seashore (GUIS).

Multibeam and swath systems have been useful in creating benthic maps in a wide range of environments (Poppe and others, 2005; Lundblad and others, 2006; Cochrane and others, 2007; Greene and others, 2007), including Channel Islands National Park (CHIS), and Glacier Bay National Park and Preserve (GLBA). High-frequency (>100 kHz) systems like the SEA Submatrix SWATHplus are ideal for shallow-water work in depths from <10 m to about 300 m. Medium-frequency (30-100 kHz) and low-frequency (12-18 kHz) systems are designed for use in water depths of 300 to 3,000 m or >6,000 m, respectively.

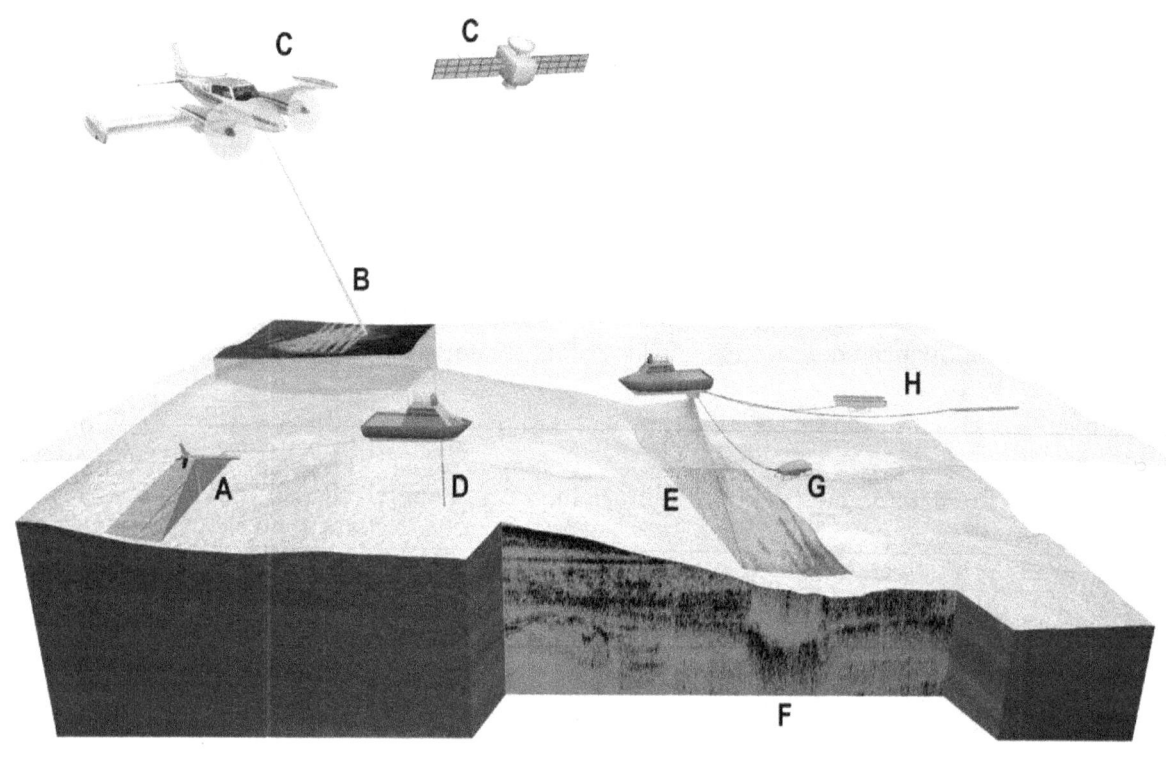

Figure 4. Diagram illustrating the basic types of remote sensing technologies with applications for benthic mapping: (A) sidescan sonar; (B) lidar; (C) color aerial or satellite imagery; (D) single-beam sonar; (E) multibeam or swath sonar; (F) seismic acquisition; (G) bottom visualization; (H) water-column data collection, and other devices. Note exaggerated differential uses between the shallow and deep ends of the diagram.

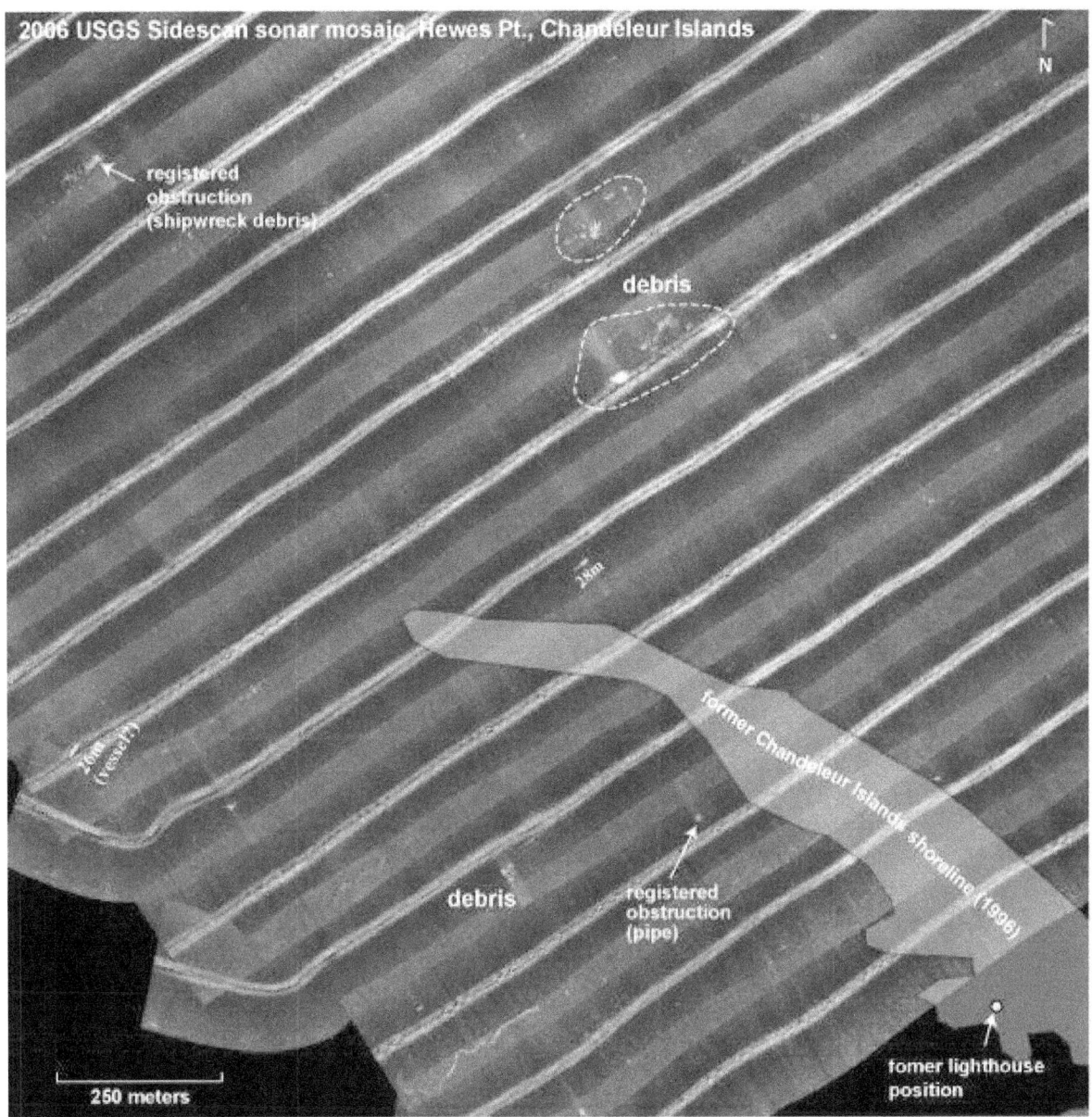

Figure 5. Example of multibeam data from the Chandeleur Islands, La. Reproduced with permission of J. Flocks (USGS).

Side-scan Sonar

Side-scan sonar operates on the same principles as multibeam sonar, but rather than being

mounted on the ship, it is typically towed below the surface behind the ship and is generally more expensive to operate. The transducers for side-scan sonar are aligned to look more sideways than downward, and the device has a "blind spot" immediately below it. Side-scan sonar is effective in shallower waters because it can detect wide areas from only a short distance above the bottom, but it is also commonly used in deeper water. This technique also allows strong detection of three-dimensional bottom features. Side-scan sonar data and backscatter information have been useful in numerous coastal applications from port security (Quintal and others, 2007) to studies of coral bleaching (Collier and Humber, 2007). An Edgetech 4100-P side-scan sonar operating at 500 kHz was used in 2008-2009 to map the lake floor around South Manitou Island at Sleeping Bear Dunes National Lakeshore (SLBE).

Single-beam Sonar

Single-beam sonar can be used to resolve depth and bottom texture immediately below the vessel. Single-beam sonars that are waveform-resolving (that is, able to determine surface textures) are also referred to as acoustic ground discrimination systems (AGDSs). Unlike multibeam or swath sonars, single-beam sonar does not need to account for the roll or pitch of the survey vessel because there is no slope determination in a single measurement.

The NPS has used an AGDS called RoxAnn at several parks for different projects, including the mapping of submerged cultural resources at BISC (fig. 6). RoxAnn uses an analog signal processing system to analyze the first echo return (E1), and also the second echo return (E2), called a multiple. The combination of the two allows determination of the distance to the seafloor and also hardness of the seabed. RoxAnn software creates a Cartesian plot grouping like values of E1 (bottom depths) and E2 (hardness) that can then be plotted on a map along the survey track to give an indication of changes in bottom types (Brown, 2007).

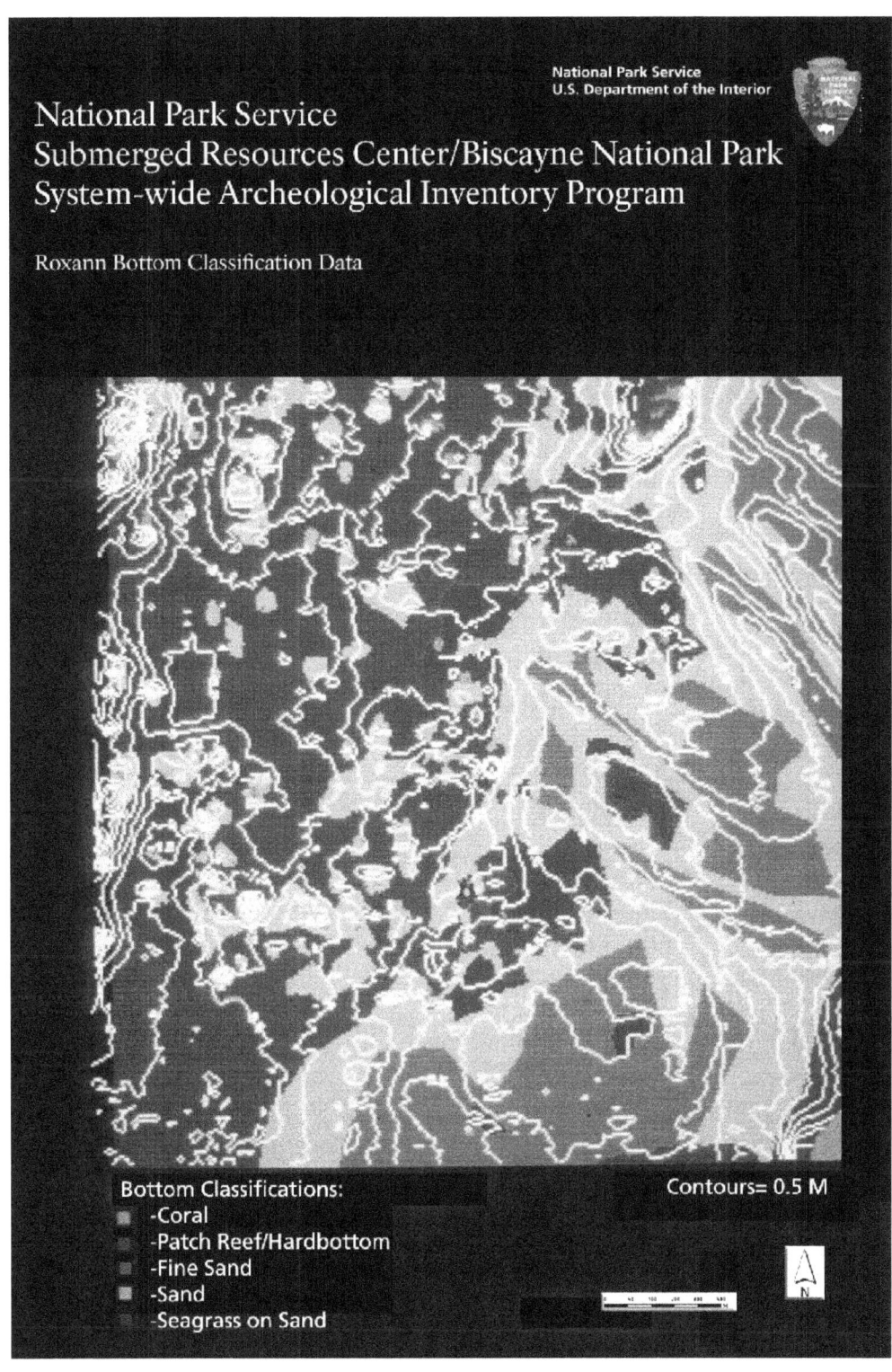

Figure 6. Interpolated classification map from RoxAnn benthic survey of Biscayne National Park. Reproduced with permission of L. Murphy (NPS).

21

Lidar

Light Detection and Ranging (lidar) can be used in optically shallow water (that is, shallow enough for the sensor to see the bottom) to collect bathymetry in the same way that sonar is used (fig. 7). The light waves from a green laser are used in a similar manner to the sound waves in sonar to measure the distance to the bottom based on a receiver measuring the two-way travel time of the pulse (Brock and others, 2004; Crane and others, 2004). Lidar operations to measure bathymetry are depth limited by the turbidity, or clarity, of the water but reach maximum reliable depths of around 25 m in clear tropical waters (Brock and others, 2004), or 2 to 3 times Secchi depth (that is, vertically measured visibility) in more turbid waters (Crane and others, 2004).

Lidar devices are typically mounted to aircraft and flown over the area of interest, though they can also be mounted on a ship instead. One benefit of lidar over sonar systems is that lidar can be used over land as well as in the water (Brock and others, 2007), allowing functionally simultaneous mapping of topography across the entire coastal zone. Another benefit is that the speed of airplanes allows them to cover great distances quickly during surveys, requiring much less time per unit area than if the mapping were done by ship. Depending on the needs, laser system, and environmental conditions, spatial resolution can range from 1 to 10 m, and vertical resolution can be 10 to 15 cm.

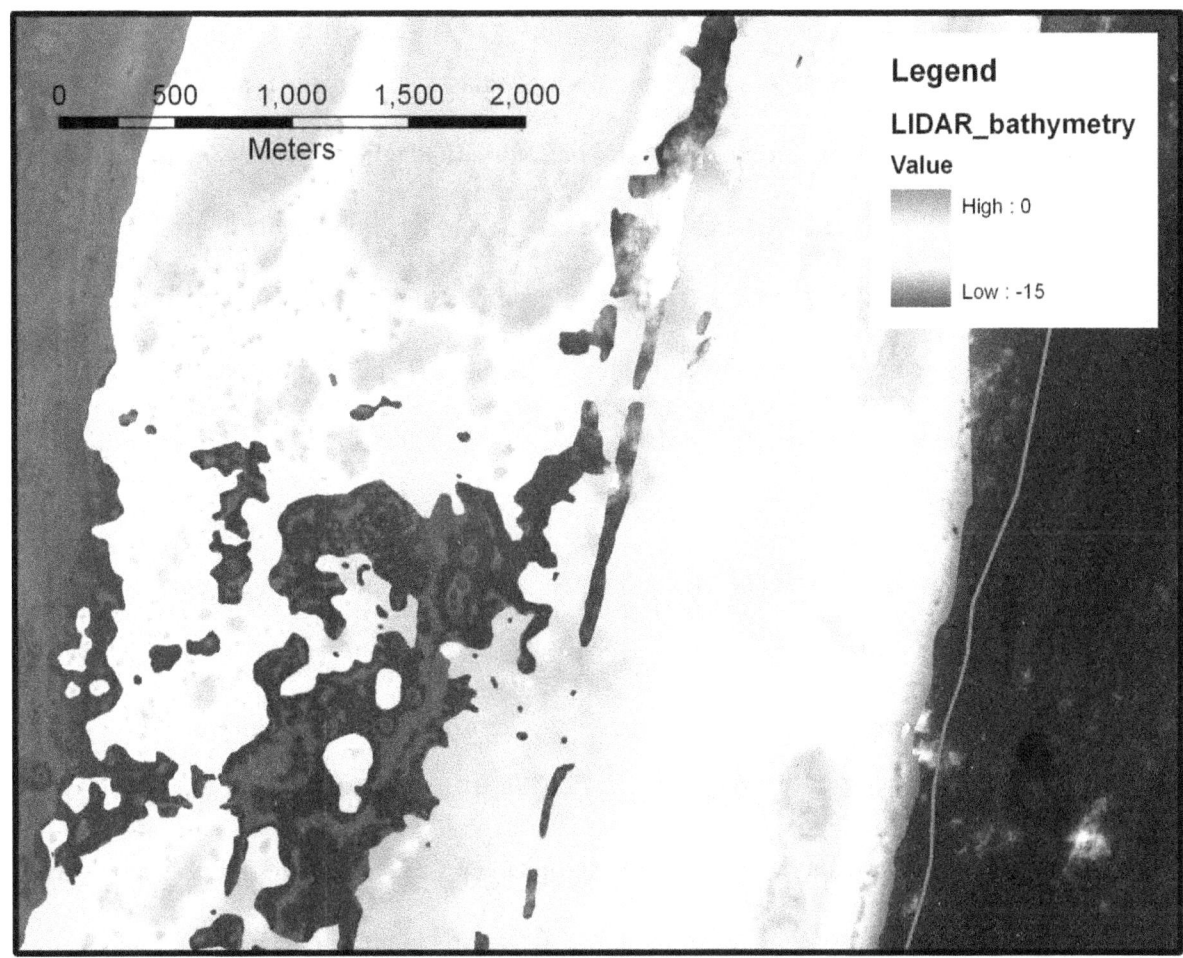

Figure 7. Lidar bathymetry of Biscayne National Park overlaid on IKONOS image. (See fig. 2 for IKONOS image and location.) Patch reefs are clearly visible as roughly circular higher elevations. Depth in meters. Red line is the Biscayne National Park eastern boundary.

Important variations between lidar systems include laser power, pulse-repetition frequency (PRF), laser-receiver capabilities, and laser spot size. There is no best combination of the variables for all missions, so the optimal system will vary based on the mapping needs. Lidar has been used extensively to map topography and bathymetry of U.S. coastlines, including numerous National Parks (for example, Assateague Island National Seashore [ASIS], BISC, and DRTO, to name a few).

23

Bottom-Visualization Systems

It is necessary to directly image the bottom to validate classifications made based on data from remote-sensing systems. Different types of bottom-visualization systems are available for this task, including simple methods, such as scuba divers, and technologically complex methods (for instance, remotely operated vehicles [ROVs] and submersibles), and each has advantages and limitations. One commonly employed method is the use of drop or towed camera systems for validation of remotely sensed data (Anderson and others, 2007; Zawada and others, 2008).

Developed by the USGS Coastal and Marine Geology Program in St. Petersburg, Fla., the Along-Track Reef Imaging System (ATRIS) is one example of a bottom-imaging camera system. ATRIS can be either mounted directly to the vessel for shallow water operations (2-10 m) or towed at limited depth for moderate-depth operations (current maximum towing depth ~27 m) (Zawada and others, 2008). The system was developed to validate remotely sensed data but has evolved into a primary data source. In recent tropical applications, the ATRIS system was useful in recording coral reef degradation and biogeologic processes typical of coral reefs (Lidz and others, 2008).

The system can be towed at speeds of up to 2.6 meters per second (m s^{-1}) (5.1 knots [kn] or 9.4 kilometers per hour [km h^{-1}]), permitting much greater coverage than classical validation using divers. The camera system records high-resolution digital images at a frame rate of 20 frames s^{-1} when vessel mounted, with a GPS location stamp tied to each image for very accurate spatial image placement (fig. 8). To adjust for light absorption at moderate depth, the system is configured with LED lights. This system has been successfully used to produce benthic image mosaics in the coral reef environment of BISC and DRTO (Lidz and others, 2008).

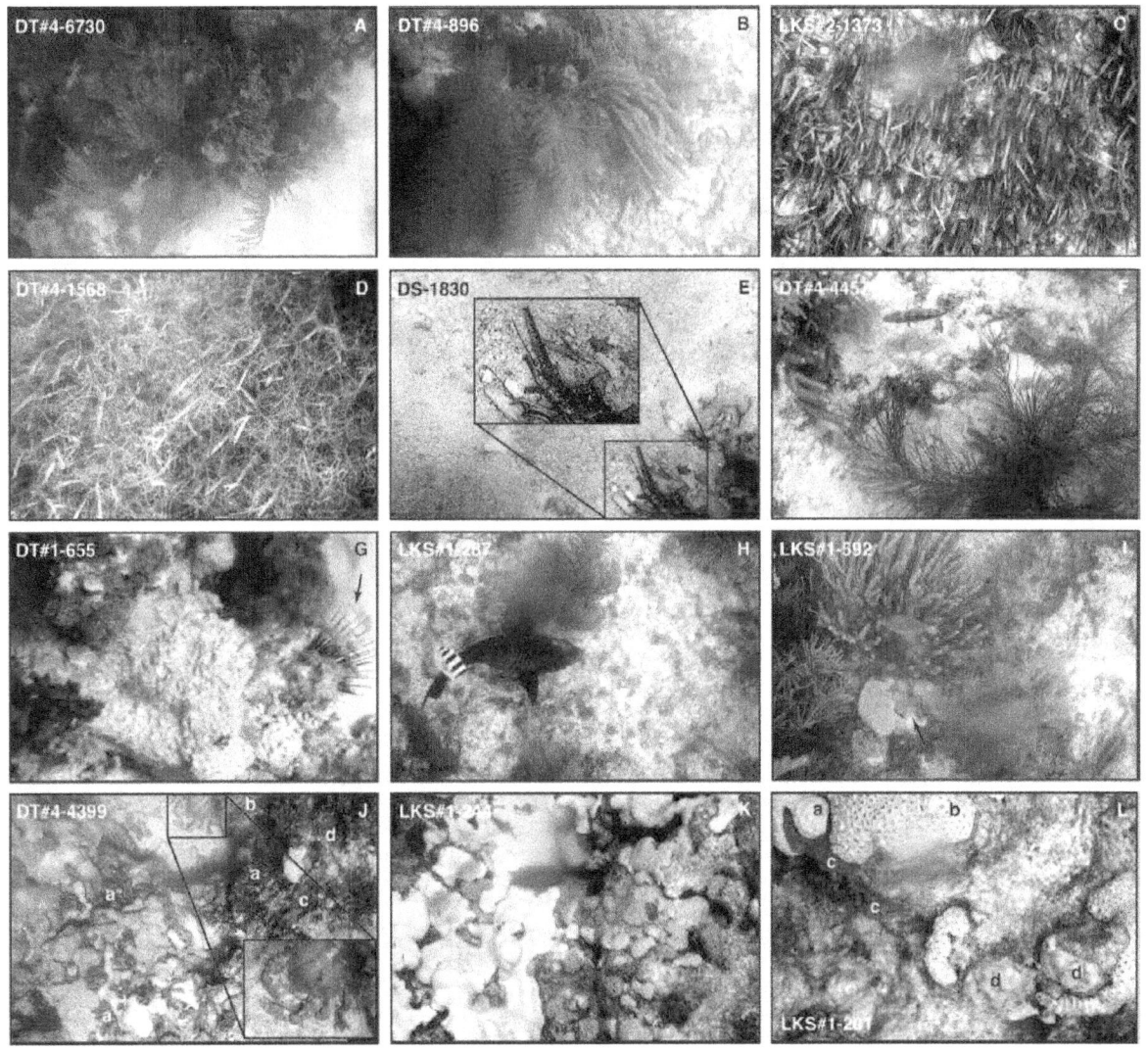

Figure 8.   ATRIS imagery from Dry Tortugas National Park and Looe Key Sanctuary (Florida Keys). Reproduced with permission from Lidz and others (2008).

Two other bottom-visualization systems are built and operated by the Bedford Institute of Oceanography (BIO) in Canada. Towcam is a towed video camera system designed to be deployed 2 to 4 m above the bottom and towed at 4 to 8 km h^{-1} (2-4 kn). With a working depth of 150 m, Towcam can record continuous video of a swath about 1 to 2 m wide. Towcam also includes a digital still camera with a strobe that can record one high-resolution digital still image every 3 to 4 s (Gordon and others, 2007).

A second bottom-visualization system operated by BIO is the Videograb system, which is a hydraulic bottom grab with mounted video cameras. The operator can select the precise sampling area and validate a successful grab before retrieving the instrument. The video camera is slightly forward looking to assist the operator's depth perception (Gordon and others, 2007).

In many environments, the joint application of Towcam and Videograb provides a solution for detailed confirmation of benthic habitats. Other bottom-visualization systems are in development at BIO.

Table 1 illustrates recommended mapping techniques based on certain environmental conditions.

Table 1. Selecting mapping technologies based on ambient conditions.

Conditions	Recommended Mapping Technology	Data Collected
Optically shallow waters with a high-contrast bottom	Satellite or airborne color imagery	high spatial resolution color images of bottom cover and formations
	Lidar	bathymetry
	Bottom visualization	bottom cover; validation
Optically shallow waters with a low-contrast bottom	Satellite or airborne color imagery coupled with single-beam Acoustic Ground Discrimination System (AGDS)	Low-contrast images of bottom cover and features supplemented with bathymetry and bottom texture
	Lidar	bathymetry
	Bottom visualization	bottom cover; validation
Optically deep waters, depth≤10 m	Single-beam sonar or AGDS	bathymetry and bottom texture
Optically deep waters, depth>10 m	Multibeam, interferometric, or sidescan sonar	bathymetry and bottom texture

Optically shallow waters are those in which the bottom can be detected by airborne or satellite imagery. Optically deep waters are either deeper, or more turbid, than optically shallow waters, and the bottom cannot be detected by airborne or satellite visible remote sensing. Depth (Z) is important in determining the appropriate acoustic device to use, since multibeam and sidescan technologies lose efficiency in shallow waters because of the decrease in swath width with decrease in depth.

Table 2 provides a summary of cost estimates for different benthic mapping technologies.

Table 2. Comparative cost estimates for different benthic mapping technologies. These numbers are greatly affected by variables such as daily ship operations costs, and the like. Costs for most of the ship-dependent instruments can be greatly reduced by combining surveys.

Technology	Estimated Acquisition Time (days)	Estimated Processing Time (days)	Estimated Total Cost** ($/km^2)
IKONOS	*	30	$240
Aerial photography	*	60	$340
Single-beam depth = 5 m	20	30	$3,200
Single-beam depth = 50 m	20	30	$3,200
Multibeam/sidescan depth = 10 m	53	110	$7,970
Multibeam/sidescan depth = 50 m	13	30	$2,120
Bottom visualization (ATRIS) depth = 20m	4	10	$670
Lidar	*	45	$1,100

* The estimated acquisition time for satellite and aerial imagery is highly dependent on the weather and the satellite queue. Image acquisition is very quick, but it may require 3-6 months to have the opportunity to acquire the image.

** Estimated costs are based on the following: IKONOS: modeled on Biscayne National Park (~675 km^2) and 10 days of field validation; aerial: modeled on Biscayne National Park (~675 km^2) and 10 days of field validation; single-beam: estimated at 5-m depth and 50-m depth for 100 km^2 and a line spacing of 100 m (equivalent to 1,000 line km), ship operations cost was estimated at \$1,700/day and ship speed was estimated at 5 kn; multibeam: estimated at 10-m depth and 50-m depth for 100 km^2 and line overlap of 30 percent, ship operations cost was estimated at \$3,000/day and ship speed was estimated at 5 kn; bottom visualization: estimated at 20-m depth for 100 km^2 and a line spacing of 1,000 m (equivalent to 100 line km), ship operations cost was estimated at \$550/day and ship speed was estimated at 5 kn; lidar: based on actual cost of 2008 acquisition and processing of lidar over ~330 km^2 of Biscayne National Park; working days: 8-hour days were used for all calculations except for field operations (validation and live aboard vessels), which were calculated based on a 12-hour day; processing time: reflects only the number of working days (for example, 5-day work week), multiply by 7/5 to estimate actual calendar time for processing; salaries: calculated at \$50/hr for electronic and GIS technicians, and \$65/hr for scientists; travel: calculated at \$1,000 per person plus hotel and per diem based on GSA rates for Miami; hotel and per diem were not included in liveaboard ship estimates.

Magnetometers

Magnetometers are particularly useful in the mapping of partially or fully buried submerged cultural resources (for instance, shipwrecks, artifacts lost overboard from ships, and so on.) (Clausen and Arnold, 1976). Magnetometers work by measuring very small anomalies in the Earth's magnetic field caused by the presence of ferrous metal, or unevenness in sediment packing resulting from in situ artifacts. Many magnetometers are able to detect variations on the order of 1 nT (1 nanoTesla = 1 gamma).

Magnetometers are generally towed 20 to 40 m behind the ship to reduce the influence of the ship's magnetic field on the data. The specifications vary from instrument to instrument. The NPS Submerged Cultural Resources Center uses a proton precession magnetometer with a survey line spacing of about 30 m, which provides sufficient coverage to identify shipwrecks and other large artifacts. The NPS successfully uses a magnetometer in most pre-disturbance surveys of suspected submerged cultural sites, including the *H.L. Hunley* Civil War-era submarine (NPS Submerged Cultural Resources Unit, 1998). Instrument measurements are processed by a computer and used to render contour maps with intervals 2 nT or 5 nT.

Geographic Information Systems (GIS) and Classification

A geographic information system (GIS) is not just a software package for viewing maps; it is the software that allows visualization, manipulation, and interpretation of geospatial data. The primary advantage of GIS over a traditional paper map is the ability to simultaneously evaluate multiple layers (for example, bathymetry, geomorphology, biotic cover, and so on) with respect to spatial distribution. Most GIS platforms, such as ArcGIS, Earth Resources Data Analysis System (ERDAS) allow manipulation of the mapped layers to include operations such as merging or splitting layers. This permits creation of new map layers based on a collection of specific attributes.

Post-Processing, Interpretation, and Validation

Post-processing of the data can be the most expensive and time-demanding step of the mapping process, depending on the acquisition technology. Post-processing describes any steps that may be applied to remotely sensed data files to adjust, or correct, selected attributes, such as georectification, radiometric corrections (for example, atmospheric or water-column corrections), sun-glint reduction, contrast enhancement, pan-sharpening, or any other form of value-added processing of the original data. Post-processing often requires proprietary and technical computing software, such as ENVI (*http://www.ittvis.com/ProductServices/ENVI.aspx*) or MatLab (*http://www.mathworks.com/products/matlab/*). Some technologies, such as satellite imagery and aerial photography, may require relatively little post-processing, whereas many acoustic techniques demand intensive post-processing to derive a quality product.

Interpretation of post-processed data produces the draft thematic (classification) map. Classification can be accomplished in three ways: unsupervised classification, supervised classification, and visual interpretation. Unsupervised classification applies algorithms with few user-determined variables and no training (Irvin and others, 1997; Chauvaud and others, 1998). Supervised classification applies functions that depend on user-defined training regions (that is, regions with a confirmed classification) (Cochrane, 2008). By indicating that a particular pixel or set of pixels represents a particular thematic class, the algorithm builds a profile to use to classify the rest of the dataset. Visual interpretation is a process of manual class separation by the user and is much more time consuming than either unsupervised or supervised classification.

Validation can be both time and resource intensive, with the exception of some surveys, such as with bottom-visualization systems, where the primary data type is somewhat self-validating. In deep-water surveys, various validation techniques can be accomplished almost simultaneously with the remote sensing survey. For example, a multibeam acoustic survey could simultaneously tow a bottom-visualization system, or at least periodically (or strategically) use a drop camera, bottom grab, or ROV to verify the benthic components. Using the same platform to collect the primary and validation data at the same time greatly increases cost efficiency. Where satellite or aerial imagery are the primary data, validation by a separate survey is unavoidable. In such cases, the most accurate validation is accomplished when the imagery and the validation survey (for example, bottom visualization or diver surveys) are collected within the shortest possible time interval.

Validation can also be performed by proxy. This is common with the use of high-resolution aerial photographs to validate the classification of satellite imagery. In this case, if the quality of the aerial imagery is sufficient for clear identification of the desired features, then it can be used to accurately validate the lower resolution satellite imagery. Proxy validation, when properly applied, can be used as a way to reduce the time and resource costs of a field-validation survey (for example, diver survey).

Validation should be designed to provide statistically significant results. Validation of only two points in an area with high spatial or temporal variability does not provide a statistically useful comparison. Likewise, validation of a survey with hundreds of mapped units at a spatial resolution of 900 m^2 (for example, Landsat satellite imagery), but each unit tested at 1 m^2 (for instance, drop camera or diver meter-square surveys) likely does not accurately capture the variability within the original mapping units. Careful forethought and validation-survey design can avoid the production of statistically useless results and avoid the expense of further validation.

Recommended NPS Benthic-Mapping Protocol

The NPS SBMP workshop in June 2008 brought together benthic-mapping experts as well as NPS resource managers and I&M coordinators. The following sections reflect the

31

combined recommendations from the NPS SBMP workshop. Workshop details can be found in Moses and others (2010).

Recommended NPS Benthic-Classification Scheme

No presently existing benthic-classification scheme entirely meets the needs of the NPS. Developing a new, solely NPS servicewide benthic classification system would delay the mapping phase of the SBMP considerably and would face significant challenges. The recommended strategy is to adopt an available classification scheme, rather than recreate one, but ensure that it meets NPS needs.

The Coastal and Marine Ecological Classification Standard (CMECS) Version III developed by NOAA and NatureServe (Madden and others, 2008; Madden and others, 2009) is under review as a national coastal habitat classification standard with the Federal Geographic Data Committee (FGDC). The FGDC accepted the proposal and started the review process. The Marine and Spatial Data Subcommittee invited NPS to participate in the review, testing, and validation of the proposed CMECS standard, which is expected to take 2 to 3 years. In its current form, CMECS Version III (Madden and others, 2009) lacks only a few capabilities essential to the NPS benthic-classification scheme, namely a submerged cultural resources classification process for sensitive data.

Recommendations:

- *Map using CMECS Version III to meet NPS needs.* CMECS will be in review with FGDC for several years, which will provide time for the NPS to test the applicability of the classification scheme and formally propose modifications. In the meantime, the NPS should proceed to map with CMECS Version III (Madden and others, 2009). This will provide important feedback to the NPS SBMP, NOAA, and FGDC.

- *Lacustrine benthic classes.* In Version III (Madden and others, 2009), CMECS does include a range of freshwater benthic classes that may be encountered in Great Lakes parks under the System: Lacustrine [LA] and Subsystems: Limnetic [1] and Littoral [2]. However, these classifications are not as well developed as the marine classifications and will benefit from further development through the FGDC review process.

- *Submerged cultural resources.* In Version III (Madden and others, 2009), CMECS does not include sufficient classes for the scope of submerged cultural resources under NPS protection. This will need to be developed further, in close collaboration with NPS Cultural Resources. Discussions with the CMECS implementation group and working group have indicated the possibility for future development of the anthropogenic geoform component to include more detailed cultural resources classifiers.

- *Internally assess the quality of CMECS maps.* The NPS will need to rigorously assess the strengths and weaknesses of CMECS Version III (Madden and others, 2009) as a benthic classification scheme during the early phases of the SBMP. Any shortcomings can be addressed with the NPS SBMP, NOAA, and FGDC to improve the classification system.

Coastal and Marine Ecological Classification Standard (CMECS)

NOAA and NatureServe developed CMECS to meet the need for a Federal standard benthic-classification system that spans the different ecological regions of U.S. coastlines and operates across scales from 1 m^2 to 10,000 km^2 (Madden and others, 2005; Madden and others, 2008). The most recent version of CMECS Version III (Madden and others, 2009) has been updated to align with current Federal standards for wetlands mapping (Cowardin and others, 1979) and vegetation mapping (Jennings and others, 2009). CMECS Version III (Madden and others, 2009) also incorporates much of the scale structure and nomenclature from a well-accepted deep-seafloor classification scheme (Greene and others, 1999; Greene and others, 2007) in the geoform component.

To classify marine and coastal environments, CMECS Version III (Madden and others, 2009) begins with a broadly defined aquatic setting called System and Subsystem. Systems (for example, nearshore, neritic, oceanic, estuarine, freshwater-influenced, and lacustrine) differ in their salinity, geomorphology, and depth. Subsystems are defined by tidal regimes (subtidal, intertidal) or, in lacustrine systems, depth (limnetic, littoral). Systems have five components that describe environmental features relevant to animal and plant habitats and communities – water column, biotic cover, surface geology, sub-benthic, and geoform (fig. 9). The Water Column Component (WCC) describes the structures, physical processes, and biology of the water column. The Geoform Component (GFC) describes the structure of the seafloor at scales from 1 m (for example, karst-solution pit [k]) to hundreds of kilometers (for example, continental shelf [8]). The Surface Geology Component (SGC) describes the composition of the surface substrate. The Biotic Cover Component (BCC) describes the biological features of the benthos at various scales. The Sub-Benthic Component (SBC) describes the structure and function of substrates and sub-benthic habitats and is presently under development. The components can be identified and mapped independently or combined, depending on the questions being asked and the mapping technology being applied.

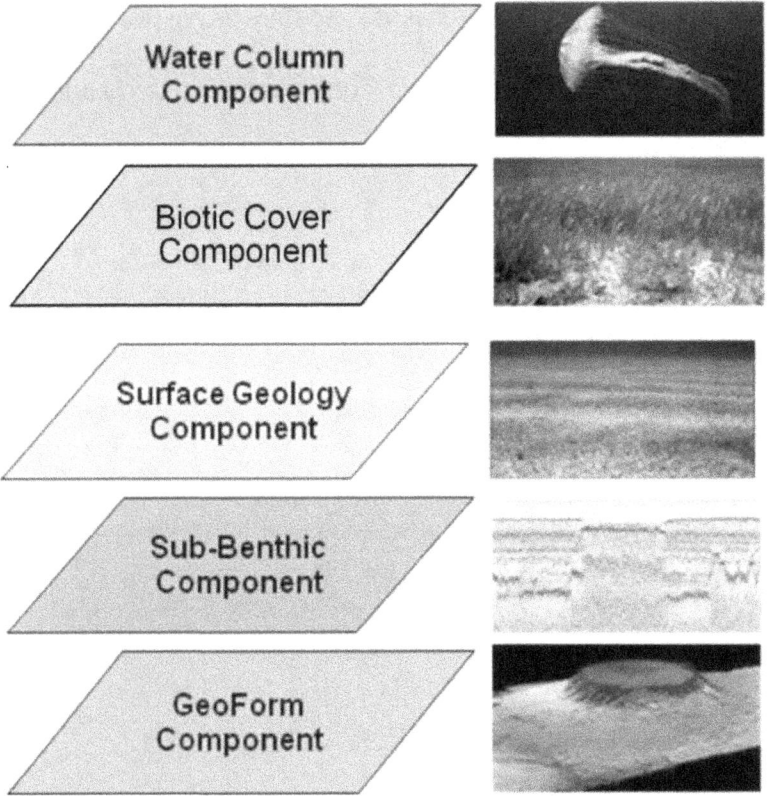

Figure 9. The five components of the CMECS Version III (Madden and others, 2009) structure.

CMECS Biotic Cover Component (BCC)

The BCC classifies the geologic and biotic cover of the substrate at different scales in a hierarchical manner. The top level of the biotic cover component is divided into "classes" such as Class:Coral Reef [CR] or Class:Faunal Bed [FB]. Below class is subclass, and both generally follow the scheme of the FGDC wetlands classification (Cowardin and others, 1979). Below subclass, there are levels (in descending order) assigned as "group" and "biotope" (fig. 10). The groups and biotopes subdivide the classification further and provide regional flexibility. BCC groups are functional organizations of organisms, such as, Biotic Group:Robust Branching Corals [rb]). Biotopes are defined by diagnostic organisms and consistent physical parameters with predictable associations to other taxa (for instance, Biotope:*Acropora palmata* reef). BCC

35

includes classifiers for faunal cover (for example, infauna, oysters) and flora cover (for example, macroalgae, seagrass). As a special case, because of their nature, coral reefs are classified in both the BCC and surface geology component.

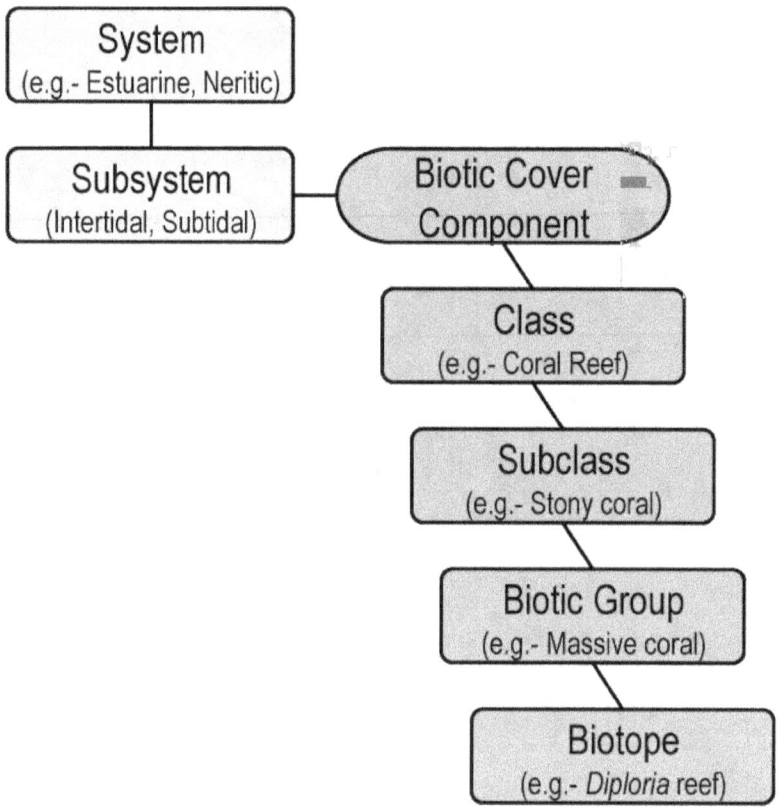

Figure 10. Diagram of CMECS Version III (Madden and others, 2009) BCC component hierarchical structure.

CMECS Geoform Component (GFC)

The GFC describes the structure of the seafloor across a range of scales from meters to thousands of kilometers. The classification framework for the GFC is derived from Greene and others (1999; 2007) but, within CMECS Version III (Madden and others, 2009), the geoform component includes a wider range of nearshore features important to the NPS. The geoform components are critical to controlling the flow of energy (currents and tides) and movement of organisms and connectivity of populations. The GFC is the three-dimensional form upon which the two-dimensional BCC and SGC are draped.

While locally specialized systems were developed to classify variable habitats in depths from 0 to 30 m, much less has been done in the often more uniform environments from 30 to 300 m (or deeper) where much of the potential habitat critical to commercial fisheries or mineral extraction exists. Greene and others (1999) presented a scheme that was modified from Cowardin and others (1979). Developed in northern latitude deeper waters, this system of classification continues to be further refined and developed for application in shallow, nearshore, and even tropical regions (Greene and others, 2007; Madden and others, 2008).

Scale and the ability to resolve geomorphic features of smaller sizes by remote sensing (for example, sonar, ROV, autonomous underwater vehicle [AUV], and the like.) are limiting factors to classifying potential habitats in areas deeper than 30 m. To address this, Greene and others (1999) divided potential habitats by scale. CMECS Version III (Madden and others, 2009) incorporates a reduced division of scale since many geoforms operate across a range of scales:

- *Physiographic Province* – Similar to a megageoform (Greene and others, 2007), a physiographic province is a large feature of similar geologic origins and structure that has dimensions ranging from a few kilometers to tens of kilometers, and larger. Examples of physiographic provinces include the continental shelf, continental slope, and abyssal plain. These features can be defined with the use of small-scale (1:1,000,000 or greater) bathymetric maps and satellite topographic images.

- *Geoform* – This unit from CMECS Version III (Madden and others, 2009) combines the mesogeoform and macrogeoform features from Greene and others (2007). Geoforms range

37

in size from 1 m to a few kilometers and include such features as large boulders, reefs, bedrock outcrops, bedforms (for example, sediment waves), small seamounts, and canyons. These morphological features can be defined using geologic or geomorphic maps and bathymetric images of the seafloor at scales of 1:250,000 or less. In addition, smaller geoforms can be defined through in situ observational data such as video and photographs, or diver surveys. Certain biogenic structures such as reefs can also be considered geoforms.

- *Anthropogenic Geoform* – CMECS Version III (Madden and others, 2009) also includes anthropogenic geoforms (fig. 11). An anthropogenic geoform ranges in size from 1 m to hundreds of meters and is by definition manmade. These features include standing artifacts such as dams and bridges, as well as remnants such as wrecks. In the case of standing artifacts, only the in-water "footprint" of the structure is mapped (for instance, only the pilings of a bridge will be indicated on the map).

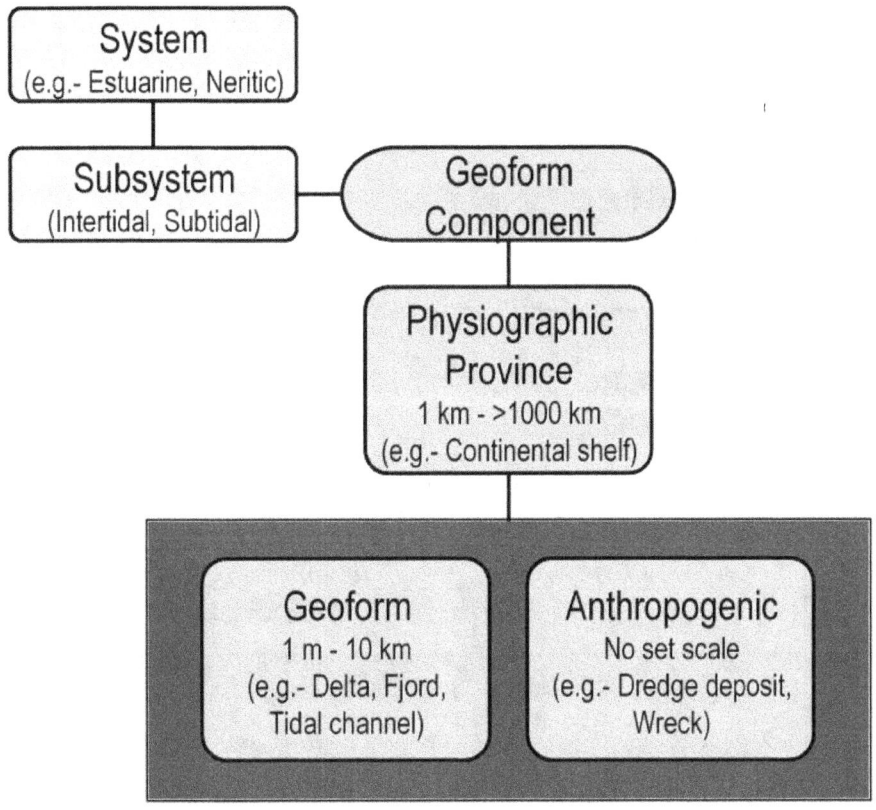

Figure 11. Diagram of CMECS Version III (Madden and others, 2009) Geoform Component semi-hierarchical structure.

CMECS Water Column Component (WCC)

Unlike the GFC and BCC, the WCC is not hierarchical and consists of a series of classifiers that can be used alone or in combination to describe the structure, physical properties, and processes of the water column (fig. 12). The first term uses the same systems as the biotic cover component such as estuarine, neritic, and so on, and classifiers can be added to describe features such as vertical stratification, currents, and so on. Because the water column is dynamic (that is, seasonal changes in temperature and salinity, tidal cycles, and so forth), only the most prominent and predictable hydrographic features should be used for mapping. The exception to this rule would be mapping of short duration but repetitive and ecologically important events such as algal blooms or upwelling.

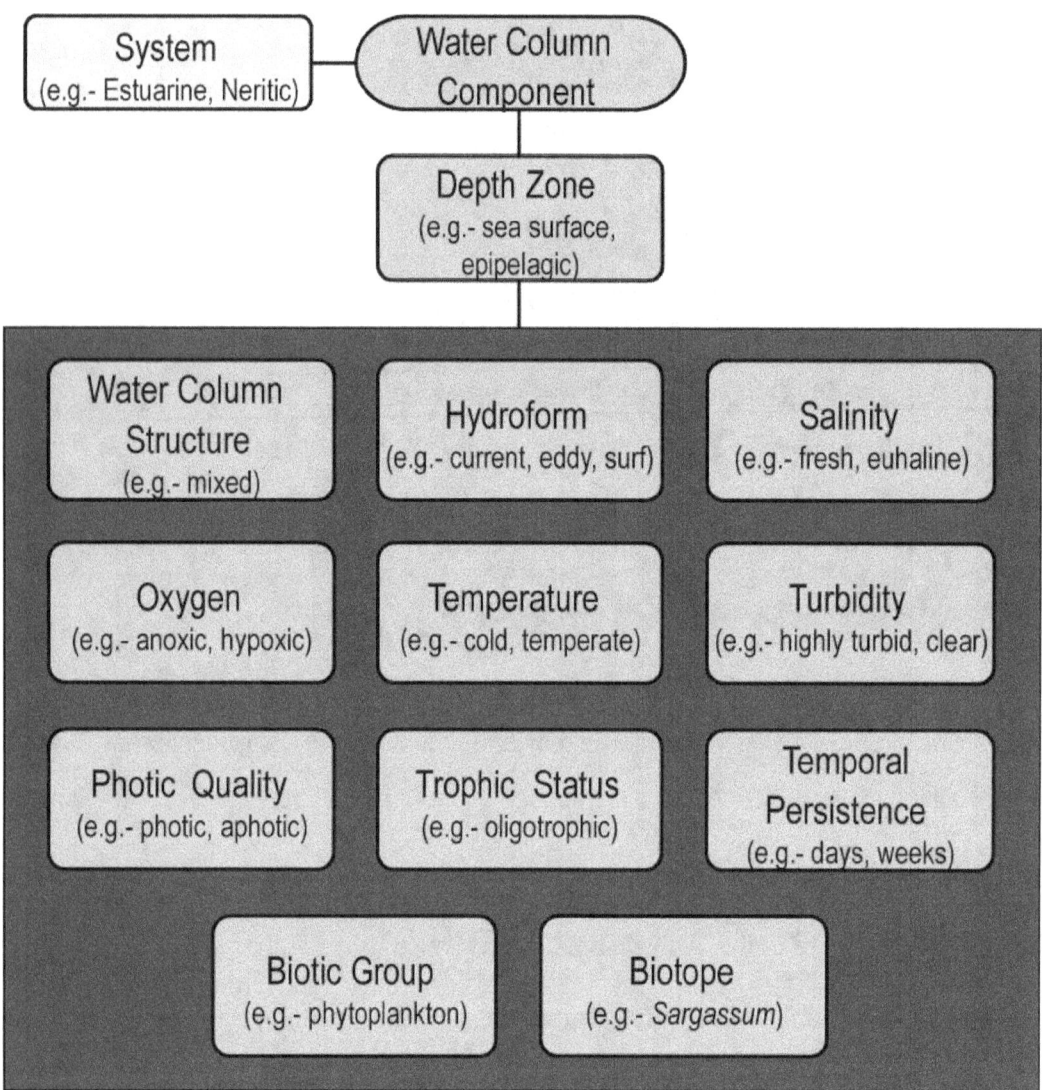

Figure 12.   Diagram of CMECS Version III (Madden and others, 2009) Water Column Component semi-hierarchical structure.

The WCC is possibly the most flexible of the CMECS components in its application and certainly the most dynamic. Additionally, the amount of observation necessary for mapping the WCC will depend not only on the horizontal extent, but also on the depth of the water column for each park unit.

CMECS Surface Geology Component (SGC)

The surface geology component (SGC) of CMECS Version III (Madden and others, 2009) is the component that provides necessary characterization of the soft or hard substrate of the benthos. The SGC describes the upper few centimeters of soft (that is, unconsolidated) sediments and the upper surface of hard-surface geology. The SGC has been specifically designed to pair with the BCC to describe all the biotic and abiotic features of the benthic environment. This is particularly useful in coral reef environments where the coral reef fauna described by the BCC are often intimately linked to the surface geology by their nature. The SGC is being further refined in cooperation with the Mapping Partnership for Coastal Soils and Sediments (MapCoast; *http://www.ci.uri.edu/projects/mapcoast/*).

CMECS Sub-Benthic Component (SBC)

The sub-benthic component (SBC) describes the structure and function of coastal and marine soils and sediments. The SBC considers soils and sediments in one group of the upper 15 cm and a second group in the zone below 15 cm. The SBC provides additional information regarding the infauna, texture (for example, grain-size distribution), composition, and other characteristics. This component can be sampled using remote-sensing equipment, such as acoustic sensors, video, and (or) still imagery, and grab and (or) core samples. Complete classification of this layer may require use of multiple tools and sampling scales. Like the SGC, the SBC is being further refined in cooperation with the Mapping Partnership for Coastal Soils and Sediments (MapCoast; *http://www.ci.uri.edu/projects/mapcoast/*).

CMECS Coding Conventions

CMECS Version III has coding conventions that allow the unique identification of thousands of habitats. Here follow several examples taken directly from CMECS Version III (Madden and others, 2009).

The CMECS "common code" begins with System and Subsystem to describe a broad aquatic setting, then defines strings from each of the five CMECS components, separated by an underscore (_):

- The s: string defines the surface geology component (SGC)

- The b: string defines the biotic cover component (BCC)

- The u: string defines the sub-benthic component (SBC)

- The g: string defines the geoform component (GFC)

- The w: string defines the water column component (WCC)

The code sentence can incorporate strings for all components but (for brevity) eliminates strings for which no data exist. The common code structure is defined as:

- System.Subsystem_**s** : Surface Geology Class.Subclass.Group.Modifier_**b** : Biotic Class.Subclass.Group.Biotope.Modifier_**u** : Sub-Benthic Class.Subclass.Group.Modifier_ **g** : Physiographic Province.Geoform1.Geoform2.Anthrogeoform.Modifier_**w** : Water Column Hydroform.Biotic Group.Biotope.Modifier

- EXAMPLE 1: Estuarine subtidal, substrate cannot be resolved, with *Zostera* Biotic Group and *Zostera marina* biotope:

  - ES.1_b:AB.3.zs.*Zost mar*

- EXAMPLE 2: Estuarine subtidal sand substrate with *Zostera* Biotic Group and *Zostera marina* biotope in a GFC Shoreline/Littoral Physiographic Province [10], with Lagoon [n], and Sandbar [sl] Geoforms:

- ES.1_s:UB.2_b:AB.3.zs.*Zost mar*_g:10.n.sl

CMECS BCC Example

DRTO has been mapped by NOAA using IKONOS satellite imagery and their coral reef classification scheme. Maximum mapped depths extend to around 20 m in most areas of the map due to water clarity. Figure 13 is a translation, or "crosswalk," directly from the NOAA classification polygons. Mapping with CMECS initially could possibly change the geometry of polygons in some areas because of slight differences in class and subclass definitions.

All classes on the map fall into the nearshore [NS] system, which is limited to open marine waters 0 to 30 m deep (fig. 13). The subsystem for all the mapped classes is subtidal [1], and the biotic cover falls into the classes coral reef [CR] and aquatic bed [AB]. For example, sand patches code out as nearshore subtidal unconsolidated bottom – sand on a continental shelf bank [NS.1_s:UB.2_g:8.m/f]. Areas of reef rubble codes out as nearshore subtidal coral reef – forereef, and faunal bed – reef rubble and mixed living stony corals on a continental shelf bank [NS.1_s:CR.5.f/FB.7_b:CR.1.mixed_g:8.m/f].

DRTO NOAA Benthic Habitats

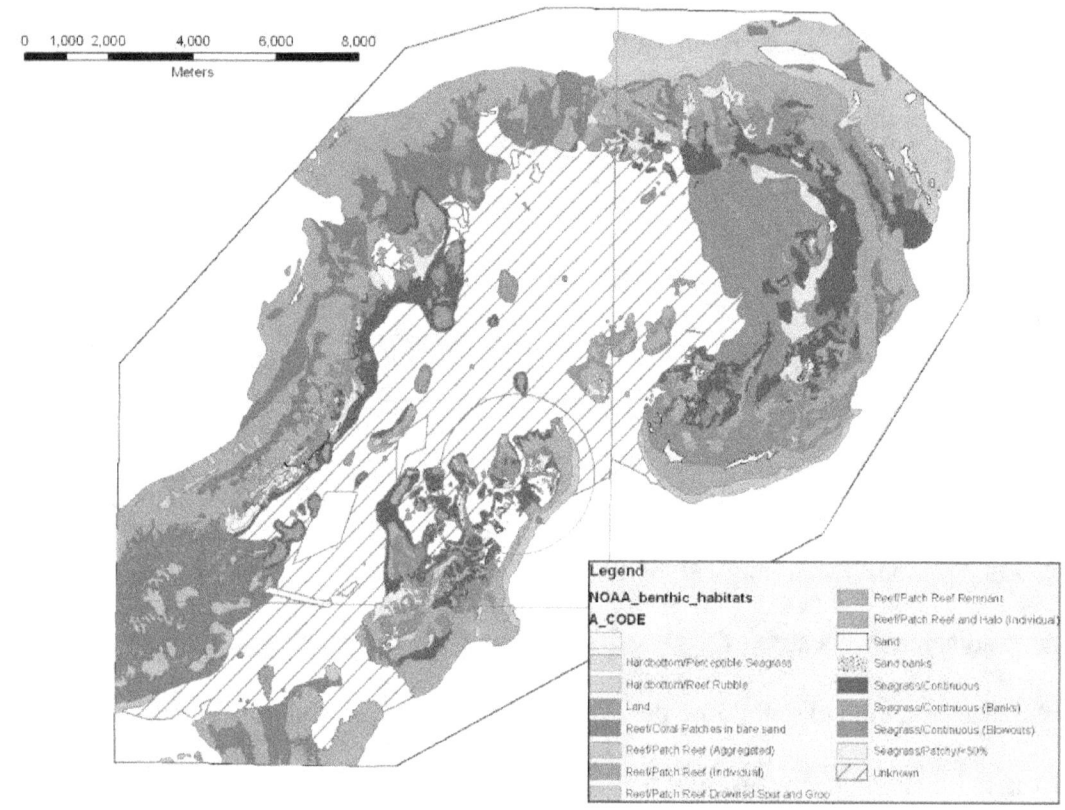

Legend

NOAA_benthic_habitats
A_CODE

Hardbottom/Perceptible Seagrass
Hardbottom/Reef Rubble
Land
Reef/Coral Patches in bare sand
Reef/Patch Reef (Aggregated)
Reef/Patch Reef (Individual)
Reef/Patch Reef Drowned Spur and Groo

Reef/Patch Reef Remnant
Reef/Patch Reef and Halo (Individual)
Sand
Sand banks
Seagrass/Continuous
Seagrass/Continuous (Banks)
Seagrass/Continuous (Blowouts)
Seagrass/Patchy/<50%
Unknown

DRTO CMECS Biotic Cover Component

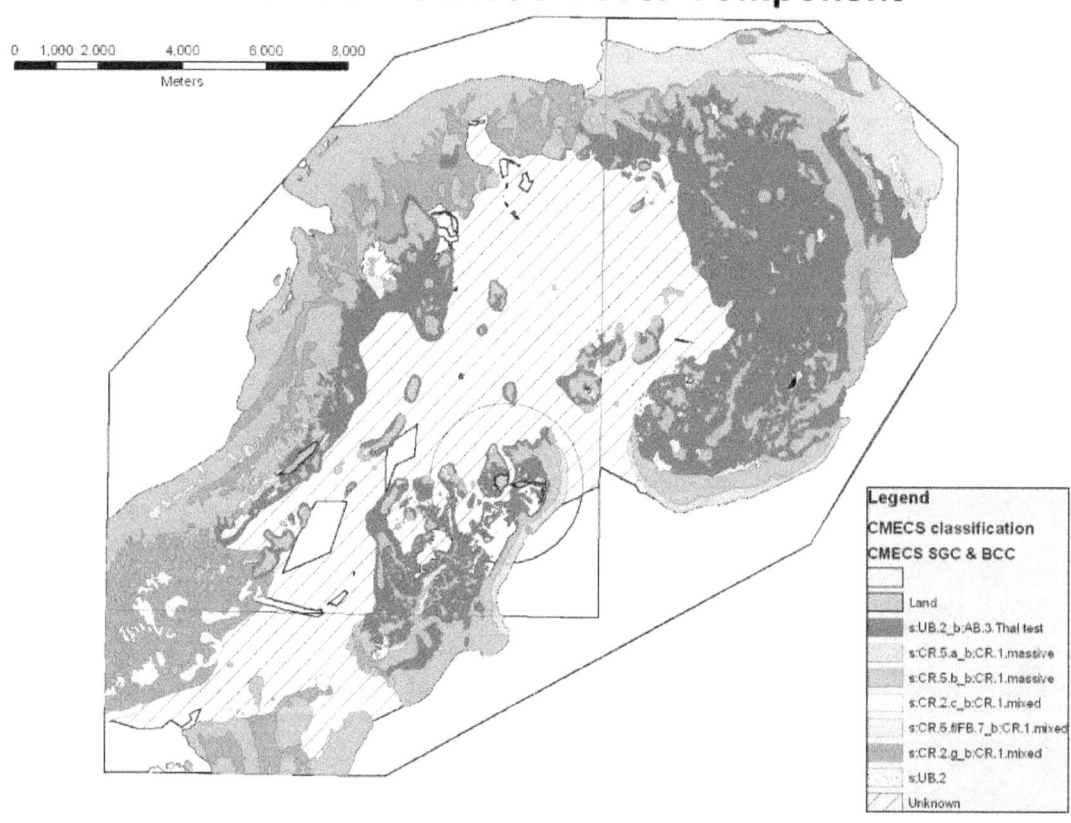

Legend

CMECS classification
CMECS SGC & BCC

Land
s:UB.2_b:AB.3.Thal test
s:CR.5.a_b:CR.1.massive
s:CR.5.b_b:CR.1.massive
s:CR.2.c_b:CR.1.mixed
s:CR.5.f/FB.7_b:CR.1.mixed
s:CR.2.g_b:CR.1.mixed
s:UB.2
Unknown

44

Figure 13. CMECS Version III (Madden and others, 2009) Biotic Cover Component (BCC) map of Dry Tortugas National Park (DRTO) ("cross-walked" from the NOAA benthic habitat map). Top: NOAA coral reef benthic habitat map. Bottom: "Cross-walked" map. The legend omits CMECS system and subsystem code for nearshore subtidal [NS.1_], which would prefix the indicated codes, and the geoform component code for continental shelf [8] and bank [m/f] that would add a suffix of [_g:8.m/f] to all indicated codes since these are constant in DRTO. For example, the complete code for the seagrass [AB.3] (*Thalassia testudinum*)-dominated areas on an unconsolidated bottom [UB] of sand [2] (green) would be: [NS.1_s:UB.2_b:AB.3.*Thal test*_g:8.m/f]. No WCC or SBC codes could be "cross-walked" based on the information provided in the original NOAA map. A key difference between the maps is the reduction in classes; the CMECS map uses only one class for seagrass instead of the four used in the NOAA map.

Servicewide Protocols

Not all of the recommended protocols for benthic mapping in NPS units need be applicable servicewide. However, certain overarching components of the SBMP do need to be uniformly addressed servicewide.

Geospatial One-Stop (GOS), the GOS "Marketplace," and Other Collaborative Groups

There is a critical need at the servicewide level to leverage partnerships and share geospatial data. Geospatial One-Stop (GOS; *http://geodata.gov*) is the centralized clearinghouse for geophysical data, maps, and projects for the Federal agencies. GOS provides a single location where scientists, managers, and the general public can download data or map products. Rather than actually store all the data locally, GOS maintains metadata and links users to the original data to avoid storage issues from needless data duplication.

One section of GOS called the "Marketplace," and identified by a tab at the top of the home page, is intended for leveraging partnerships. The GOS Marketplace provides a forum for Federal agencies, academics, and private industry to post planned surveys or place a request for data. If properly used, GOS Marketplace could greatly reduce unnecessary overlap in data acquisition between or even within agencies.

Interagency collaboration is also available through the Interagency Working Group on Ocean and Coastal Mapping (IWG-OCM). The IWG-OCM was formed by the Joint Subcommittee on Ocean Science and Technology (JSOST) to increase efficiency in the Nation's ocean and coastal mapping community. The IWG-OCM is designed to avoid duplication of effort and increase communication between agencies involved in ocean and coastal mapping.

- *NPS participation on the IWG-OCM and in the GOS Marketplace.* The NPS currently maintains a representative who is directly involved with mapping coastal parks as a member of the IWG-OCM (as of the time of publication, Roger M. Johnson, NPS Cartographer). NPS I&M directors can be tasked with ensuring that NPS data needs and planned mapping operations are posted to the GOS Marketplace in a timely fashion. Both actions are critical to leverage partnerships for mapping and to avoid unnecessary duplication of effort.

- *Improve access to NPS data.* Making servicewide data available through the NPS Data Store and GOS as soon as projects are completed will guarantee that the data are available to park unit managers as quickly as possible. Additionally, if NPS shares its resources openly, other agencies may be more likely to explore cost-saving partnerships with the NPS.

Gap Analysis

A critical problem facing the NPS is gaps in mapping and inventory data. Gaps can be either geospatial (that is, unmapped parks or sections of parks), thematic (for example, a completed bathymetric map, but no data for the biotic cover component), or a combination of the two. Gap analysis within the ocean and coastal park units is a priority for the early phase of the

46

SBMP. At the servicewide level, there should be summaries of regional and network gap analyses would be useful for I&M coordination.

- *Gather initial summaries of gap analyses.* Regional and network I&M coordinators can provide initial gap analyses and mapping priorities for their park units and make this information available to the NPS Ocean and Coastal Resources Branch (OCRB). The gap analyses will support the mapping plans during the early phases of SBMP.

- *Provide a computerized or Web-ready form for gap analysis.* The NPS can provide regional and network coordinators with a spreadsheet or internal Web form to make gap analysis reports more uniform. This will increase efficiency in the servicewide decision process by making gap comparison possible between regions, networks, and park units.

Mapping Process

A protocol for the mapping process will streamline mapping operations and make it easier to assess the progress of each program. Mapping begins with a thorough investigation of existing data, an announcement of the project timeline and goals, and then follows with data collection, interpretation, and final product delivery.

- *Data mining.* Once a park unit is identified as a mapping priority and a proposal has been approved, extensive data mining will help to avoid duplication of effort. Sending a survey to park managers will help to determine their needs (fig. 14).

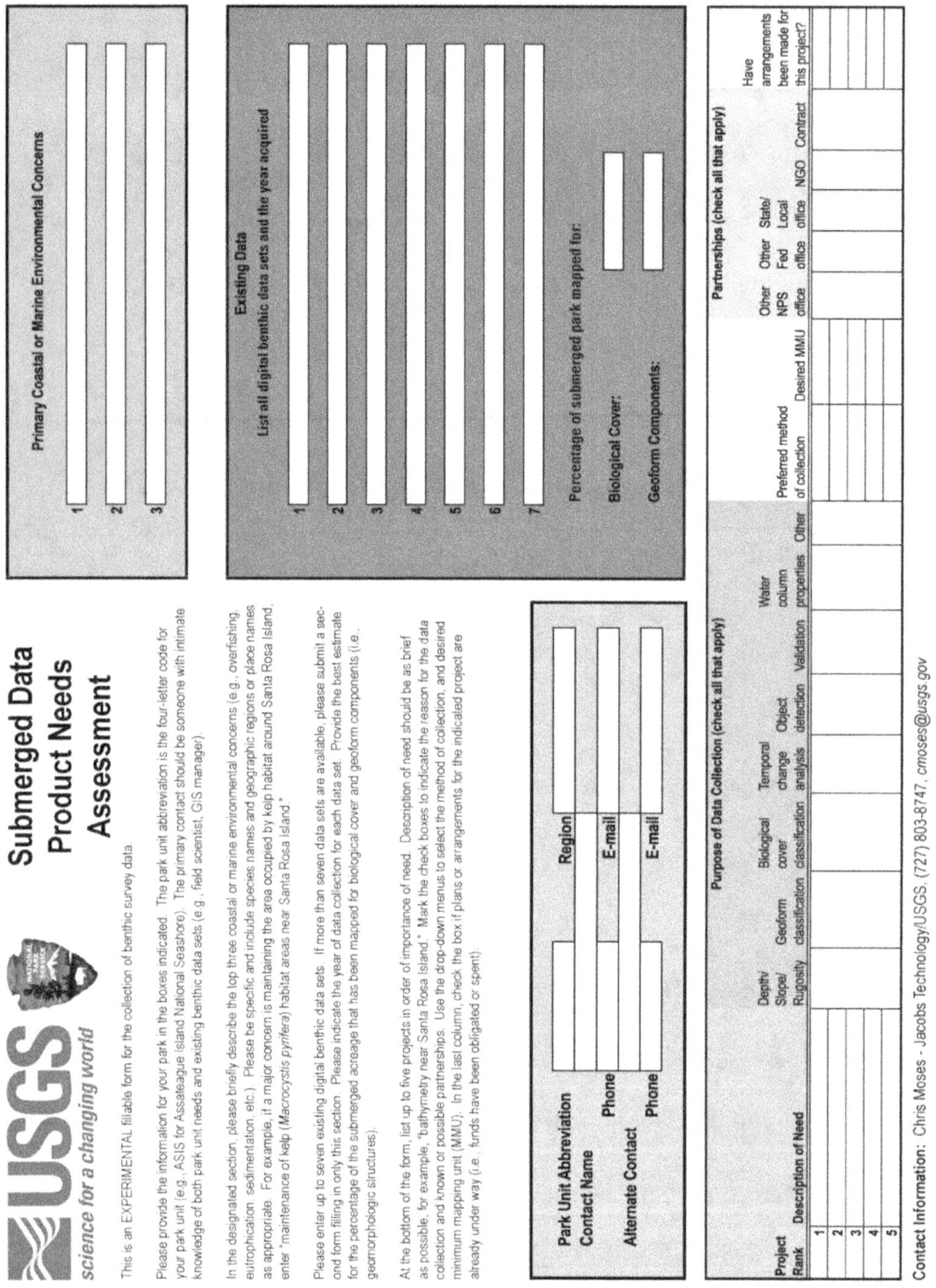

USGS *science for a changing world*

Submerged Data Product Needs Assessment

This is an EXPERIMENTAL fillable form for the collection of benthic survey data.

Please provide the information for your park in the boxes indicated. The park unit abbreviation is the four-letter code for your park unit (e.g., ASIS for Assateague Island National Seashore). The primary contact should be someone with intimate knowledge of both park unit needs and existing benthic data sets (e.g., field scientist, GIS manager).

In the designated section, please briefly describe the top three coastal or marine environmental concerns (e.g., overfishing, eutrophication, sedimentation, etc.). Please be specific and include species names and geographic regions or place names as appropriate. For example, if a major concern is maintaining the area occupied by kelp habitat around Santa Rosa Island, enter "maintenance of kelp (*Macrocystis pyrifera*) habitat areas near Santa Rosa Island."

Please enter up to seven existing digital benthic data sets. If more than seven data sets are available, please submit a second form filling in only this section. Please indicate the year of data collection for each data set. Provide the best estimate for the percentage of the submerged acreage that has been mapped for biological cover and geoform components (i.e., geomorphologic structures).

At the bottom of the form, list up to five projects in order of importance of need. Description of need should be as brief as possible, for example, "bathymetry near Santa Rosa Island." Mark the check boxes to indicate the reason for the data collection and known or possible partnerships. Use the drop-down menus to select the method of collection, and desired minimum mapping unit (MMU). In the last column, check the box if plans or arrangements for the indicated project are already under way (i.e., funds have been obligated or spent).

Primary Coastal or Marine Environmental Concerns

1
2
3

Existing Data
List all digital benthic data sets and the year acquired

1
2
3
4
5
6
7

Percentage of submerged park mapped for:

Biological Cover:

Geoform Components:

Park Unit Abbreviation | **Region**
Contact Name
Phone | **E-mail**
Alternate Contact
Phone | **E-mail**

		Purpose of Data Collection (check all that apply)										Partnerships (check all that apply)					
Project Rank	Description of Need	Depth/ Slope/ Rugosity	Geoform classification	Biological cover classification	Temporal change analysis	Object detection	Validation	Water column properties	Other	Preferred method of collection	Desired MMU	Other NPS office	Other Fed office	State/ Local office	NGO	Contract	Have arrangements been made for this project?
1																	
2																	
3																	
4																	
5																	

Contact Information: Chris Moses - Jacobs Technology/USGS, (727) 803-8747, *cmoses@usgs.gov*

Figure 14. Draft NPS-USGS benthic-mapping needs questionnaire. This sheet is a fillable PDF that limits certain responses via pull-down menus and can be electronically submitted. This particular version has been distributed to NPS personnel at Assateague Island National Seashore, Channel Islands National Park, and Sleeping Bear Dunes National Lakeshore for testing as part of a pilot gap analysis project.

- *GOS Marketplace and IWG-OCM announcement.* Announcing anticipated projects early will help optimize opportunities for partnerships. Information from the aforementioned network and park gap analysis and needs questionnaires can be used to leverage partnerships in GOS Marketplace.

- *Scoping meeting.* Meetings held at the network or park unit level prior to mapping should include regional and network I&M managers, park superintendents, leading park unit physical and biological scientists, and the external collaborators directly involved in the mapping process (that is, technical experts, cooperating Federal and State agencies, and the like). The goals of the mapping project will help determine extent of the area to be mapped for each individual park.

- *Data collection.* Collaborate with technical experts and partners to acquire the data efficiently, avoiding duplication or the need for re-acquisition when at all possible.

- *Data processing.* Post-processing of the data can be the most time-demanding step of the process, depending on the acquisition technology. Some technologies, such as satellite imagery and aerial photography, require relatively little post-processing, whereas many acoustic techniques demand intensive post-processing to derive a quality product.

- *Data interpretation.* This step produces the draft thematic (that is, classification) map. Three fundamental processes are available to create the draft map.

  - *Unsupervised classification.* Unsupervised classification uses algorithms with few user-determined variables and no training pixels (Irvin and others, 1997; Chauvaud and others, 1998). This can be useful in cases where the user is unsure about the number of classes that should be mapped or is unsure if certain classes are separable (for example, can sparse seagrass and dense seagrass be accurately discriminated with the given sensor?).

49

These algorithms will provide a graphical representation of the ability of the acquisition instrument and data quality to reliably separate thematic classes.

- *Supervised classification.* This process uses algorithms that depend on user-defined training pixels (that is, pixels with a confirmed classification) (Cochrane, 2008). By indicating that a particular pixel or set of pixels represents a particular thematic class, the algorithm builds a profile to classify the rest of the dataset. Supervised classification will perform very poorly when attempting to distinguish classes with low separability (for instance, attempting to distinguish two species of seagrass using a true-color satellite image).

- *Visual interpretation (VI).* Visual interpretation is much slower per unit area than either unsupervised or supervised classification because it proceeds by on-screen class separation by the user. No algorithms are required, and a priori knowledge of the environment can be used to determine class boundaries and classification without direct evidence in the data.

- *Validation of the draft map.* It is best to perform validation by direct sampling, such as using scuba divers or remotely operated cameras (for example, drop- or tow-cameras, or ROVs). However, direct sampling is resource intensive and, depending on the environment, may not be safe or practical (for instance, in turbid, high-energy water). When necessary, proxy validation (that is, using one remote-sensing product to validate another) can be effective.

- *Revision of the draft map.* After validation, a revised thematic map is created. This is the first map that can be circulated beyond anyone directly involved in the mapping process.

- *Expert review and publication.* Internal and external experts are given a 30-day minimum period to review the revised draft map for thematic accuracy and general utility. Assigning official map numbers will allow all final maps to be properly cataloged. A final version is then submitted for publication as the key deliverable of the SBMP.

- *Data Archive.* All digital data are archived in a common-use, nonproprietary format. The archived data include the raw instrument data as well as all the value-added products, including the final reports. The archived data are made available through a variety of online data warehouses, such as Geospatial One-Stop, NPS Data Store, to name a few.

Inventory and Map Completion

Incomplete inventories or maps of a given park unit are to be expected at any time during the mapping process. However, finalized inventories or maps that largely indicate features as "unknown" have reduced utility for management applications. With rare exceptions for extenuating circumstances, the SBMP considers a given park unit inventory complete when no more than 10 percent of any map component such as bathymetry, biotic cover, and so forth, is classified as "unknown."

Map Accuracy

The NPS SBMP needs servicewide standards for minimum acceptable accuracy. There are three primary types of accuracy for maps: (1) thematic, (2) geospatial, and (3) topological.

- *Thematic.* This is the accuracy of what is on the bottom compared to the class identified on the map at any given point. For example, for a polygon labeled as nearshore subtidal coral reef – reef rubble, at the minimum mapping unit (MMU), most of the points sampled should be reef rubble, not seagrass or healthy reef.

- *Geospatial.* This is the positional accuracy of the polygon borders and placement. For example, the placement of a polygon that outlines reef rubble should accurately reflect the

51

location and shape of the reef rubble. Geospatial accuracy directly impacts thematic accuracy.

- *Topological.* This is the accuracy of the class definition relative to what is found on the bottom. For example, creating only a "patch reef" class, but no corresponding classes for reefs that are not patch reefs, results in poor topologic accuracy. Broad classes (for example, coral reef, aquatic bed) generally have high topological accuracy, but they have decreased utility for management. Alternatively, overly specific topologies with improved management utility (for instance, 10 percent live hermatypic coral with algae, or 30 percent *Thalassia* sp. on fine carbonate sand) tend to decrease thematic accuracy in the final map because of their highly specific definitions.

Each of three categories has independent measures of acceptable accuracy. The minimum acceptable accuracy is ultimately determined by the impact that error would have on proper management. Thematic and geospatial accuracy can only be assessed on a map product; topological accuracy is addressed prior to mapping.

- *Thematic.* Accuracy is 100 percent at the highest level (that is, the broadest level of classification) and 80 percent at the most detailed level mapped. Accuracies of less than 80 percent indicate either that there is a problem with the technology and its application or that maps are being produced beyond capabilities to render accurate maps. Managers should be able to select a field location with confidence that no fewer than 8 out of 10 sites will be thematically correct.

Proper thematic accuracy assessment procedures ensure the production of accurate maps. Improperly performed thematic accuracy assessments often lead to inflated reports of map accuracy, which will ultimately result in poor management decisions. Good accuracy assessments take into account the spatial resolution of the sensor and the class separability as part of their design. Overall thematic accuracy can be measured in a matrix where the diagonal represents properly classified points or pixels, and the off diagonals represent misclassified points or pixels (fig. 15). This alone is not a sufficient measure of thematic accuracy since a random classification will have some number of correctly classified points.

In addition to the assessment of overall thematic accuracy by using a matrix, thematic accuracy can also be measured using the Tau coefficient (T) (Ma and Redmond, 1995; Mumby and others, 1997). A T statistic can be easily understood, since it represents the percentage of correctly classified points or pixels beyond what would be expected from random chance. For example, a score of 0.85 indicates that 85 percent more pixels are correctly classified than are expected by random chance. Thus, the combination of an overall accuracy assessment matrix with a T statistic gives a stronger indication of thematic accuracy than an accuracy assessment alone (Mumby and others, 1997).

- *Geospatial.* This is primarily limited by the spatial resolution and positional accuracy of the sensor and the MMU. Generally, with raster data, error is expected to be less than 50 percent of the horizontal resolution of the instrument and less than 25 percent of the size (vertical and horizontal planes) of the features intended to be resolved.

  - *Horizontal Accuracy.* The USGS national map accuracy standard is that no more than 10 percent of randomly selected validation points should be misplaced by more than 1/50 of an inch on a 1:20,000 scale map (U.S. Geological Survey, 1999). This translates to no more than 10 percent of test points being in error by more than 400 inches (10.2 m) on the ground. At coarse MMUs (for example, 30 m, 1 acre, and so on), precision must be better than less than 50 percent of the MMU.

- *Vertical Accuracy.* The USGS national map accuracy standard is that no more than 10 percent of randomly selected validation points should be in error by more than half the contour interval (U.S. Geological Survey, 1999). This translates to no more than 10 percent of test points being in error by more than half of the vertical resolution of the instrument. For some lidar measurements in shallow clear water, a hypothetical acceptable error would be for less than 10 percent of validation points to be vertically incorrect by more than approximately 7 cm.

- *Topologic.* Topology needs to be specific enough for management decision support and able to be merged upward to fit entirely in the superior-level class.

	Classified as (percent)				
	DLS	SLS	SG	SSG	Sand
DLS	**66.7**	3.7	25.9	3.7	0
SLS	0	**53.8**	23.1	23.1	0
SG	1.3	0	**84.2**	14.5	0
SSG	0	0	0	**92.9**	7.1
Sand	0	0	0	0	**100**

Figure 15. Example accuracy assessment matrix for Landsat satellite imagery in a coral reef environment. DLS = dense live substrate; SLS = sparse live substrate; SG = seagrass; SSG = sparse seagrass. The row headers indicate what the benthic cover actually was, and the column headers indicate how the benthic cover was classified. A value of 100 percent along the diagonal (for example, sand) indicates 100 percent accurate thematic classification for that particular class. Reproduced with permission from Moses and others (2009).

Final SBMP Deliverables and Products

The SBMP will develop a servicewide standard for deliverables so that all parks receive equivalent products. Uniform deliverables will help ensure equity of management utility for each park unit.

- *Hard-copy maps.* Park unit managers and resource scientists take hard-copy maps to the field and mark them up as necessary. Network and park managers indicated that this is one of the most important deliverables (Moses and others, 2010).

  - Full-color maps on durable paper (for example, water resistant for field use) at a size of about 36 x 24 inches or equivalent.

  - Minimum features include a map of:

    - Bathymetry (fig. 16)

    - At least one of the following layers:

      - Biotic cover component (BCC)

      - Surface geology component (SGC)

      - Geoform component (GFC)

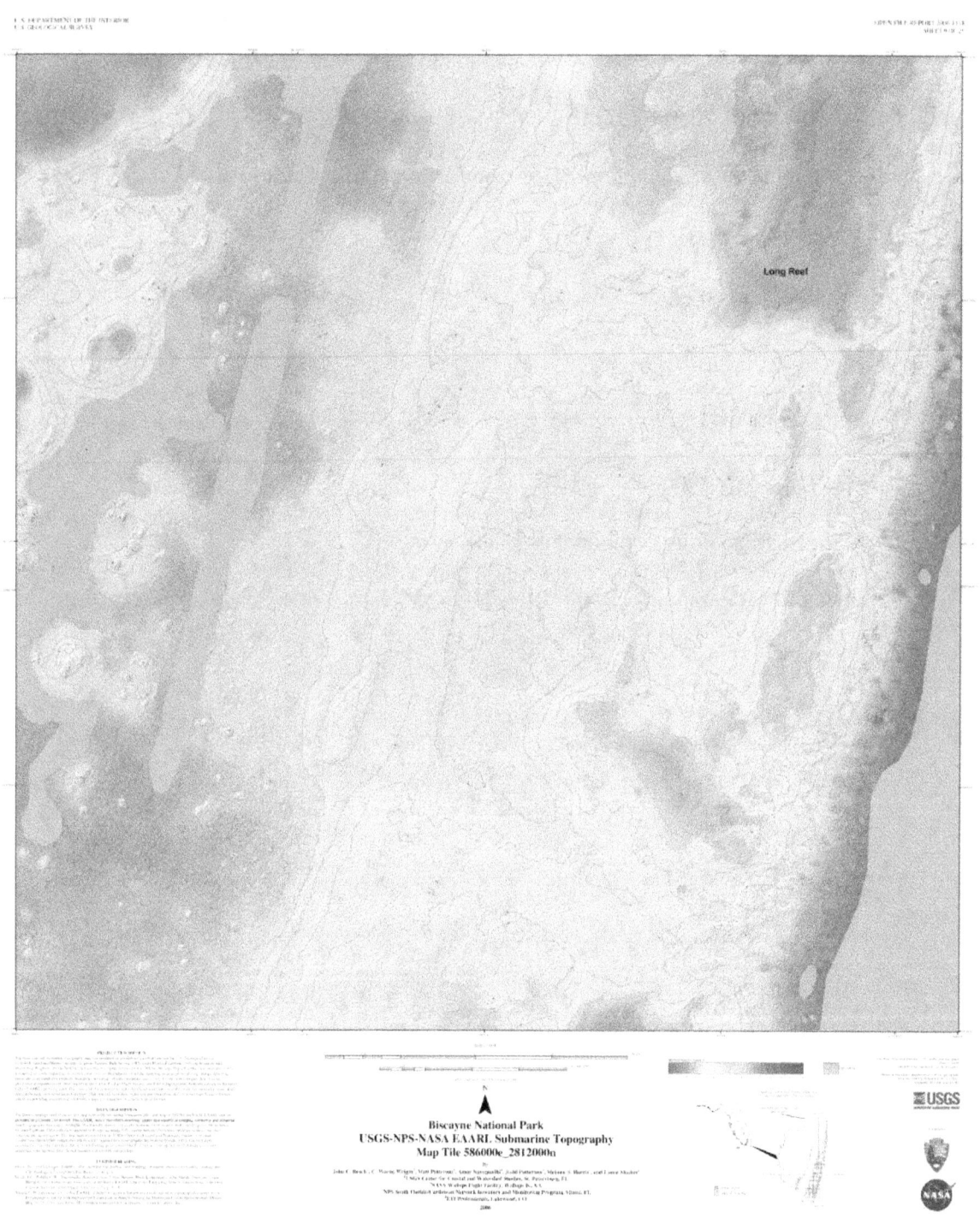

Figure 16. Example of lidar bathymetry map from Biscayne National Park (ready-to-print PDF tile). The full-sized, ready-to-print file has a page size of 34 x 44 inches. Reproduced with permission from Brock and others (2006a).

- *Bound report.* This is intended for rapid and easy access to, or distribution of, information related to the benthic systems for a given park unit (see Gibbs and others, 2007). This includes at a minimum:
  - Study area geologic and ecologic framework
  - Discussion of regional and local physical oceanography
  - Methods and data collection
  - Results (detailed by category as applicable)
  - Maps and figures representing every data layer available for the park unit.
- *DVD with report and printable maps.* A DVD with digital resources is a useful archive of benthic-mapping products and includes at a minimum:
  - All GIS and map data (for example, shapefiles, raster data, metadata, and the like)
  - PDF or equivalent digital format of the bound report
  - Large (24 x 36 in or greater) ready-to-print PDF files (or equivalent) of each map in the bound report
  - Large (24 x 36 in or greater) ready-to-print PDF tiles (or equivalent) of maps with sufficient detail to be enlarged to that scale (see fig. 16)
- *Publicly available online resources.* Sharing information collected for each park unit is important. Online resources include:
  - HTML viewable and downloadable PDF or equivalent formats of a summary of the bound report with the most pertinent text, figures, maps, and metadata.
  - Downloadable GIS files, such as shapefiles, raster data, metadata, for the core maps (that is, park boundaries, bathymetry, benthic cover, and so on).

- Downloadable maps formatted for display in Google Earth® (for instance, KML and KMZ formats).

- Carefully screened and approved submerged cultural resources prior to inclusion in the public online resources.

Region, Network, and Park Unit Scale Protocols

The results of the SBMP workshop held in June 2008 stressed maintaining need-based mapping flexibility demanded by managers with protocols adapted to regional, network, and park unit scales (Moses and others, 2010). The wide range of NPS park locations and the diversity of management concerns make it difficult to apply a truly identical process to each park unit. Instead, submerged-habitat mapping will be standardized at a servicewide level, and the elements will be controlled at the park, network, or regional levels.

Minimum Mapping Unit (MMU)

The minimum mapping unit (MMU) represents the highest uniform spatial resolution for a map product. For example, an MMU of 30 m would indicate the ability to resolve features of 30 m or greater. Any features ≤30 m would be classified based on dominance within a 30-m pixel. MMU must be addressed at the network or park unit level because it is not practical to set a servicewide standard (for example, 30 m) when such a measure would be too fine for large parks and too coarse for small parks or in sections of parks with high spatial variability.

Apparent structure and organization of spatially and thematically complex ecosystems, such as coral reefs, are sensitive to thematic and spatial resolution of maps. Patchy features are most strongly influenced, whereas more coherent or linear features are not influenced much, if at all (Kendall and Miller, 2008). MMU also directly impacts measures of ecosystem health such as species diversity. Although habitat richness is not strongly influenced, diversity measurements are. Additionally, MMU influences the apparent size-frequency distribution within populations and forces the merging of many habitat types (for example, "patch reef" may be merged upward to "patch reef and sand"). Small-area habitats are lost at coarse scale but are replaced by mixed-class descriptors (Prada and others, 2008).

- *Geophysical data and MMU.* Any geophysical data (that is, satellite, sonar, and the like) will be collected, archived, and made available at the maximum instrument spatial resolution. For example, if a park can map with two otherwise identical sensors, cost permitting, the sensor with the higher resolution will be used. If the data are acquired at a higher resolution than the MMU, they will not be downgraded to the MMU when they are included in the deliverables.

- *Determining the MMU for a park unit.* MMUs are determined by the inventory needs and geographic extent of each park unit. Specifically, managers will determine the MMU not by the instrumentation available for mapping, but rather by the most important features to be inventoried in that park unit. If only relatively coarse features are to be resolved, a park unit could potentially save significant financial and time resources by not having to map at a higher spatial resolution.

Mapping Bathymetry

Following the servicewide mapping guidelines (above), bathymetry will be the first map layer completed for each park unit. Bathymetry is to be mapped at the highest resolution possible, but does not need to be mapped in all sections of the park with the same technology. For example, lidar could be used in sections of a park with shallow, clear water, and swath sonar could be used in deeper sections (fig. 17). In the case of shallow, turbid waters, single-beam sonar systems often perform better than lidar and are cheaper to operate than multibeam sonar in most cases. The technology applied will depend on the particular conditions in each area to be mapped.

- *Units.* Units are preferred to be reported in meters (m) relative to the WGS 84 map datum, but other recognized units (for example, feet, fathoms) and datums are acceptable as long as they are internationally recognized and clearly indicated as such on the map and in the metadata.

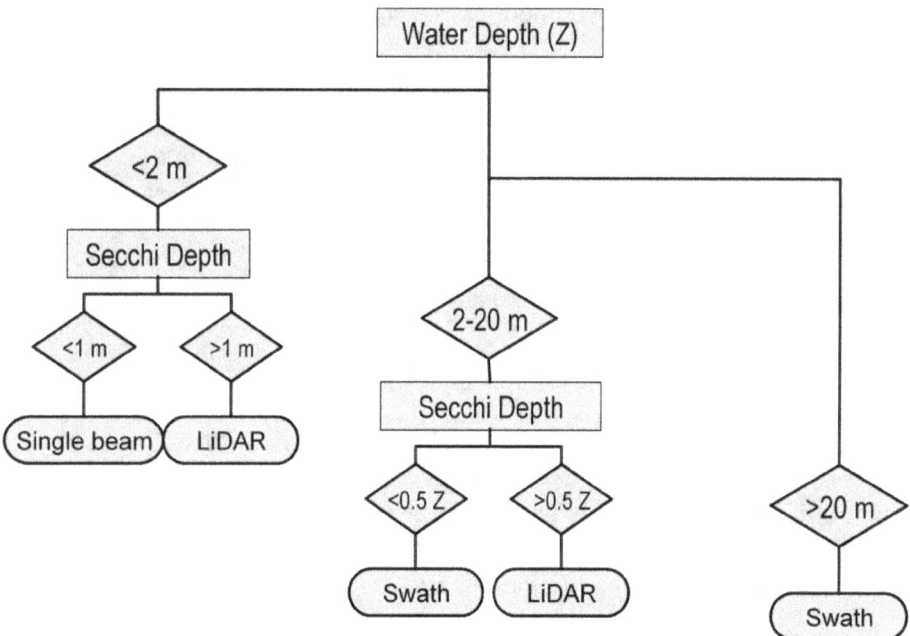

NOTE: Area to be mapped is also critical in determining which method is optimal. Cost for swath data acquisition increases exponentially in shallow areas compared with the same square area in deeper water.

Figure 17. One possible decision matrix for bathymetric mapping in park units.

Mapping the Geoform Component

In many cases, the GFC can be almost completely mapped using the bathymetric map, and thus is the logical next step. The physiographic province for any park unit should be known through previous work and knowledge of regional geologic structure. In most cases, with the exception of park units like Buck Island Reef National Monument (BUIS), which spans an exceptional depth range from the shore to 1,700 m, the GFC physiographic province will be the same for the entire park unit (for example, continental shelf). The geoform should be able to be mapped using remotely sensed data with a resolution of 1-10 m and subsequent validation by bottom visualization or divers. Because the physiographic province should be common knowledge, the minimum acceptable level of mapping for the GFC is to the geoform with any applicable modifiers. Features smaller than 1 m are not realistic to map for SBMP or most other management purposes and have thus been excluded from CMECS.

Swath sonar is particularly useful for mapping the GFC. Both bathymetry and substrate texture are acquired simultaneously, allowing production of three map layers (bathymetry, GFC, and SGC) from a single field campaign.

Mapping the Biotic Cover Component (BCC)

The guiding principles lean in favor of the importance of biotic communities. As such, even small amounts of living cover define the BCC attribute as one of the biotic classes (for example, coral reef [CR], faunal bed [FB], aquatic bed [AB], and so on) rather than abiotic classes, which reside in the SGC, despite the fact that by percent area, the abiotic class may be the dominant feature. In fact, the BCC and SGC are engineered to be applied simultaneously to describe both the biological and physical attributes of an environment.

61

The biotope attribute is designed to allow expansion as necessary for regional needs. As the application of CMECS grows, so will the biotope attribute list. The list incorporated in this document and in CMECS Version III (Madden and others, 2009) are not to be considered final.

Mapping the Water Column Component

The WCC is the CMECS component with the fewest restraints to classification. The first two characters must represent the system and depth zonation. Beyond that, classifications may proceed based on the water-column parameters that are known.

* *WCC attribute codes.* At this time, codes are in the process of being assigned for each attribute.

Concluding Remarks

A consistent, Servicewide Benthic Mapping Program will allow proper inventory and management of the NPS submerged natural and anthropogenic resources. The recommended benthic mapping approach depends heavily on the evolving design and status of CMECS. As CMECS is more broadly applied, revisions will no doubt improve the applicability to the NPS SBMP. At the moment, with CMECS beginning the FGCD review process, there is an opportunity for the NPS to take an active role in developing CMECS as a more useful tool for the NPS.

Acknowledgments

The authors gratefully acknowledge Emily Klipp for invaluable assistance in management of the manuscript reviews and very thorough text editing. The authors thank the technical and editorial reviewers of this report. A joint collaboration between the USGS Coastal and Marine Geology Program and the NPS Inventory and Monitoring Program funded this investigation as a component of the Decision Support for Coastal Science and Resource Management project (*http://coastal.er.usgs.gov/remote-sensing/*).

APPENDIX 1. CMECS component codes (Version III, Madden and others, 2009)

Table 3. System and subsystem codes.

System	Subsystem
Estuarine [ES]	Subtidal [1]
	Intertidal [2]
Nearshore [NS]	Subtidal [1]
	Intertidal [2]
Neritic [NE]	
Oceanic [OC]	
Freshwater-Influenced [FI]	Subtidal [1]
	Intertidal [2]
Lacustrine [LA]	Limnetic [1]
	Littoral [2]

Table 4. Biotic Cover Component (BCC) codes.

This is not a substitute for the information contained in the full CMECS documentation (Madden and others, 2009).

Class	Subclass	Biotic Group	Biotope
Faunal reef [FR]	Mollusk reef [1]	Oyster reef	*Ostrea* reef, *Crassostrea* reef
		Mussel reef	*Mytilus* reef, *Modiolus* reef
		Gastropod reef	Vermetid reef, *Crepidula* reef
	Worm Reef [2]	Worm reef	*Phragmatopoma* reef, *Sabellaria* reef
Coral reef [CR]	Living stony coral communities [1]	Robust branching corals	*Acrophora palmata* reef
		Fragile branching corals	*Acropora* reef, *Porites* reef, *Madracis* reef, *Oculina* reef, *Lophelia* reef, *Pocillopora* reef
		Table corals	*Acropora* reef
		Massive corals	*Diploria* reef, *Montastraea* reef, *Montipora* reef, *Porites* reef
		Plate corals	*Agaricia* reef, *Montastraea* reef
		Encrusting corals	*Millepora* reef, *Porites* reef
	Calcareous Algal Communities [2]	Rhodolith beds	*Lithothamnion* communities, *Lithophyllum* communities
		Crustose calcareous algae	
		Upright calcareous algae	*Halimeda* communities
Faunal bed [FB]	Sessile epifauna [1]	Oyster bed	*Ostrea* communities, *Crassostrea* communities
		Mussel bed	*Mytilus* communities, *Modiolus* communities
		Sessile gastropods	*Crepidula* communities, vermetid communities
		Barnacles	*Chthamalus* communities, *Balanus* communities
		Coral garden	Mixed soft coral communities, gorgonian communities
		Mixed colonizers	Virginian mixed colonizing communities, deep-water northern Gulf of Mexico mixed colonizing communities

2

Class	Subclass	Biotic Group	Biotope
		Sponge bed	*Microciona* communities, *Hyalonema* communities
		Attached anemones	*Metridium* communities
		Burrowing anemones	*Cerianthus* communities, *Edwardsia* communities
		Small tube-building fauna	*Ampelisca* communities, *Polydora* communities, *Streblospio* communities, *Paraprionospio* communities
		Larger tube-building fauna	*Chaetopterus* communities, *Lagis* communities, *Diopatra* communities, *Asychis* communities, *Asabellides* communities, *Loimia* communities
		Crinoids	*Diplocrinus* communities, *Comanthus* communities
		Hydroids	*Sertularia* communities, *Tubularia* communities
		Bryozoans	*Bugula* communities, *Celleporaria* communities
		Tunicate bed	*Didemnum* communities, *Molgula* communities
		Foraminifera	*Xenophyophore* communities
	Mobile epifauna [2]	Mobile gastropods	*Nassarid* communities, *Turritellid* communities
		Mobile crustaceans	*Pagurus* communities
		Scallop beds	*Argopecten* communities, *Placopecten* communities
		Sand dollars	*Mellita* communities, *Clypeaster* communities
		Ophiuroids	*Ophiura* communities, *Ophiothrix* communities, *Amphiura* communities
		Holothurians	*Kolga* communities, *Stichopus* communities
	Infauna [3]	Clam bed	*Macoma* communities, *Venus* communities, *Spisula* communities, *Mercenaria* communities, *Mya* communities, *Nucula* communities, *Yoldia* communities, *Mulinia* communities, *Rangia* communities, *Arctica* communities
		Tunneling megafaun	*Squilla* communities, *Nephrops* communities, *Upogebia* communities, *Callianassa* communities, *Thallassia* communities
		Small surface burrowing fauna	*Capitellid* communities, *Oligochaete* communities, *Lumbrinerid* communities, *Leptocheirus* communities
		Deposit feeders	*Nucula* communities, *Yoldia* communities, *Macoma* communities, *Maldanid* communities, *Clymenella* communities,

Class	Subclass	Biotic Group	Biotope
			Pectinaria communities
		Larger deep-burrowing fauna	*Nephtys* communities, *Nereis* communities, *Nemertean* communities
		Burrowing urchins	*Echinocardium* communities, *Lovenia* communities
		Ophiuroids	*Ophiura* communities, *Ophiothrix* communities, *Amphiura* communities
		Echiurid communities	*Urechis* communities, *Echiurus* communities
		Oligozoic	Anoxic oligozoic areas, Meiofaunal communities, Bacterial communities
Aquatic bed [AB]	Macroalgae [1]	Attached ephemeral macroalgae	Mixed ephemeral macroalgae, *Ulva* communities, *Enteromorpha* communities, *Agardhiella* communities, *Chaetomorpha* communities, *Chordaria* communities
		Rockweeds	*Fucus* communities, *Ascophyllum* communities
		Leathery red macroalgae	*Chondrus* communities
		Kelp forests	Mixed kelp communities, *Macrocystis* communities, *Laminaria* communities, *Alaria* communities
		Leathery green macroalgae	*Codium* communities
		Jointed calcareous algae	*Corallina* communities, *Halimeda* communities
		Attached crustose algae	*Hildenbrandia* communities, *Phymatolithon* communities
		Rhodolith bed	*Lithothamnion* communities, *Lithophyllum* communities
		Drift ephemeral algae	Drift *Ulva*
		Drift algae	Drift kelp communities, Drift rockweeds
	Rooted vascular [3]	*Cymodocea - Thalassia* seagrass bed	*Cymodocea filiformis* seagrass bed
			Thalassia testudinum seagrass bed
		Halodule - Halophila seagrass bed	*Halodule wrightii* seagrass bed
			Halophila engelmannii seagrass bed
		Ruppia seagrass bed	*Ruppia maritima* seagrass bed
			Ruppia maritima seagrass bed
		Zostera seagrass bed	*Zostera marina* seagrass bed

4

Class	Subclass	Biotic Group	Biotope
		Phyllospadix seagrass bed	*Phyllospadix (scouleri, torreyi)* seagrass bed
	Microbial Mat [5]	Microphytobenthos	Diatom communities, Cyanobacterial communities
		Bacterial mat	*Beggiatoa* mat communities
		Chemoautotrophic bacteria	*Thiobacillus* mat communities
Emergent wetlands [EM]	Coastal salt marsh [1]	Emergent high salt marsh	*Monanthochloe littoralis* emergent tidal high salt marsh
			Spartina patens - (Distichlis spicata) emergent tidal high salt marsh
			Spartina spartinae emergent tidal high salt marsh
			Schoenoplectus americanus emergent tidal high salt marsh
		Emergent low salt marsh	*Spartina alterniflora* tidal low salt marsh
			Juncus roemerianus tidal low salt marsh
		Emergent brackish marsh	*Amaranthus cannabinus* tidal brackish marsh
			Cladium mariscus ssp. *jamaicense* tidal brackish marsh
			Sagittaria subulata - Limosella australis tidal brackish
			Schoenoplectus pungens tidal brackish marsh
			Spartina alterniflora - Schoenoplectus robustus - Amaranthus cannabinus tidal brackish marsh
			Spartina cynosuroides tidal brackish marsh
			Typha (angustifolia, domingensis) tidal brackish marsh
Scrub-shrub wetland [SS]	Coastal salt marsh [1]	Scrub-shrub high salt marsh	*Baccharis halimifolia - Iva frutescens* tidal shrubland alliance
		Scrub-shrub tidal flat and panne	*Batis maritima* tidal dwarf-shrub high salt marsh
			Borrichia frutescens tidal shrub-scrub high salt marsh
			Sarcocornia pacifica - (Distichlis spicata, Salicornia spp.) tidal shrub-scrub high salt marsh
			Sarcocornia pacifica - (Distichlis spicata, Spartina alterniflora) tidal dwarf-shrub high salt marsh
	Mangrove [2]	Scrub-shrub mangrove	*Rhizophora mangle* tidal mangrove shrubland
Forested wetlands [FO]	Mangrove [2]	Forested mangrove	*Avicennia germinans* tidal mangrove forest

5

Class	Subclass	Biotic Group	Biotope
			Rhizophora mangle tidal mangrove forest
			Conocarpus erectus tidal mangrove forest

6

Table 5. Geoform Component (GFC) codes.

Physiographic Province	Code	Geoform (Natural)	Code	Geoform (Natural)	Code	Anthropogenic Geoform	Code
Fracture zone, spreading center	1	Apron, deep fan, bajada	A	Flank	F	Artificial reef	(a-r)
Mid-ocean ridge	2	Atoll	a	Flat, floor, seabed	f	Berm (anthropogenic)	(a-b/m)
Abyssal plain	3	Bank	m/f	Fracture, crack, crevice, notch, groove	f	Dam, dike	(a-g)
Oceanic bank (plateau)	4	Basin	h	Hole, pit, scour mark, pockmark (non-karst)	h_e	Dredge deposit/mound	(a-dm)
Continental, Island rise	5	Bay, embayment, sound, bight, fjord	q	Ice feature	i	Dredged channel, groove, trench or hole	(a-dg)
Continental, island slope	6	Beach, relic (submerged)	b	Lagoon, enclosed water	n	Drilling platform	(a-s)
Shelf break	7	Boulder(s)	h(b)	Landslide, slump	l	Harbor, marina	(a-m)
Continental shelf, island shelf	8	Canyon	c	Lava field	f_v	Jetty	(a-g)
Basin floor, borderland	9	Canyon head	c(h)	Ledge, overhang	_d	Levee (anthropogenic)	(a-o)
Coast	10	Canyon mouth	c(m)	Moraine	i m	Pier	(a-s)
Inland sea, enclosed sea	11	Channel, gully, inlet, tidal channel	g	Mound, ridge, knob	m	Seawall	(a-s/w)
		Channel bank	g/m	Overbank deposit, levee (natural)	o	Shipwreck	(a-w)
		Delta, fan	y	Pinnacle, cone	p	Trawl disturbance	(a-td)
		Depression	h	Rill (linear deposit or depression)	r	Scar/prop scar	(a-f)
		Face	i	Rock outcrop	e	Pilings	(a-s)
		Riverine estuary	er	Shoal	sl	Archaeological feature	(a)
		Rubble zone	h(b)l_h	Slough	h/g		
		Sand ripple	_r	Solution pit, sink, karst	k		
		Scarp, cliff, fault, slump scar	s	Fjord			
		Seamount	x	Sub-estuary	es		

Physiographic Province	Code	Geoform (Natural)	Code	Geoform (Natural)	Code	Anthropogenic Geoform	Code
		Seamount crown, crest, top	x(c)	Terrace, plain	t		
		Seamount base	x(b)	Terrace/plain - volcanic	t_v		
		Guyot, flat-topped seamount	x(f)	Trench (natural)	T		
		Guyot base	x/f(b)	Wall	(w)		
		Sediment/sand wave	w(w)	Vent	e		
		Sediment/sand dunes	w(d)	Tidepool	u		

Table 6. Surface Geology Component (SGC) codes.

System	Subsystem	Class	Subclass	Reef Morphology
Estuarine [ES]	Subtidal [1]	Rock bottom [RB]	Bedrock [1]	
Nearshore [NS]	Intertidal [2]		Boulder [2]	
Neritic [NE]		Unconsolidated bottom [UB]	Cobble/gravel [1]	
Oceanic [OC]			Sands [2]	
Freshwater-influenced [FI]			Muds [3]	
Lacustrine [LA]			Organic [4]	
			Shell [5]	
			Mixed sediments [6]	
			Reef rubble [7]	
		Rock shore [RS]	Bedrock [1]	
			Boulder [2]	
		Unconsolidated shore [US]	Cobble/gravel [1]	
			Sands [2]	
			Muds [3]	
		Faunal bed [FB]	Organic [4]	
			Shell [5]	
			Mixed sediments [6]	
			Reef rubble [7]	
		Coral reef [CR]	Reef lagoon [1]	Spur and groove reef [a]
			Back reef [2]	Patch reef [b]
			Reef flat [3]	Aggregate patch reef [c]
			Reef crest [4]	Linear reef [d]
			Forereef [5]	Aggregate Reef [e]
			Deep forereef [6]	Live hardbottom [f]
			Pinnacle reef [7]	Scattered coral/rock on unconsolidated bottom [g]
			Mesophotic reef [8]	
			Deep cold-water reef [9]	
			Outlier reef [10]	

Table 7. Water Column Component (WCC) classifiers.

System	Depth Zones	Water Column Structure	Salinity	Temperature	Biotic Group	Biotope
Estuarine	Sea surface	Upper (mixed) water layer	Fresh	Frozen	Phytoplankton	(many)
Freshwater influenced	Epipelagic	Pycnocline	Oligohaline	Superchilled	Zooplankton (includes icthyoplankton)	
Nearshore marine	Mesopelagic	Bottom-water layer	Mesohaline	Cold	Floating microbial mat	
Neritic	Bathypelagic	Benthic-boundary layer	Polyhaline	Temperate	Floating macroalgae	
Oceanic	Abyssalpelagic	Non-stratified	Euhaline	Warm	Floating vascular vegetation	
Lacustrine	Hadalpelagic		Hyperhaline	Hot		

Table 8. Water Column Component (WCC) condition assessment parameters.

Oxygen	Turbidity	Photic Quality	Trophic Status
Anoxic	Extremely turbid	Photic	Oligotrophic
Hypoxic	Highly turbid	Aphotic	Mesotrophic
Oxic	Moderately turbid	Seasonally photic	Eutrophic
Oxygen-saturated	Clear		
Oxygen-supersaturated	Extremely clear		

Table 9. Water Column Component (WCC) hydroforms.

Hydroforms MANIFESTATION						
Coastal water mass	Density current	Entrainment	Hydrothermal plume	Internal wave	Salt wedge	Turbidity maximum
Downwelling	Divergence	Freshwater lens	Ice	Langmuir cell	Surf	Upwelling
Convergence	Cold-core rings	Frontal boundary	Plunging current	Eddy	Surface foam	Warm-core ring
Counter current		Groundwater seep	River/stream current	Oxygen minimum	Surface wave	
Current	Gyre			Plume	Turbidity current	

10

APPENDIX 2. Ocean and Great Lake Parks with Submerged Acreage

	Park Name	NPS Region	State	Water (km²)	Coastline (km)	Depth (m)
1	Acadia National Park	NE	ME	48	84	
2	Apostle Islands National Lakeshore	MW	WI	109	248	
3	Assateague National Seashore	SE	MD & VA	126	138	
4	Biscayne National Park	SE	FL	675	80	18
5	Buck Island Reef National Monument	SE	VI	75	5	1703
6	Cabrillo National Monument	PW	CA	0.5	2	10
7	Canaveral National Seashore	SE	FL	159	39	
8	Cape Cod National Seashore	NE	MA	66	80	
9	Cape Hatteras National Seashore	SE	NC	16	246	
10	Cape Lookout National Seashore	SE	NC	79	90	
11	Channel Islands National Park	PW	CA	497	283	387
12	Cumberland Island National Seashore	SE	GA	41	48	
13	Dry Tortugas National Park	SE	FL	259	6	33
14	Everglades National Park	SE	FL	2500	250	8
15	Fire Island National Seashore	NE	NY	18	84	
16	Fort Sumter National Monument	SE	SC	0.5	2	
17	Gateway National Recreation Area	NE	NY	72		
18	Glacier Bay National Park and Preserve	AK	AK	2406	1,908	
19	Golden Gate National Recreation Area	PW	CA	15	45	
20	Gulf Islands National Seashore	SE	FL & MS	461	122	
21	Indiana Dunes National Lakeshore	MW	IN	2	40	
22	Isle Royale National Park	MW	MI	1752	544	
23	Jean Lafitte National Historical Park and Preserve, Barataria Preserve	SE	LA	0.7	29	
24	Kalaupapa National Historic Park	PW	HI	8	2	

25	Kaloko-Honokohau National Historic Park	PW	HI	2	3	
26	Katmai National Park & Preserve	AK	AK	2688	800	
27	National Park of American Samoa	PW	AS	13	53	
28	Olympic National Park	PW	WA	61	92	
29	Padre Island National Seashore	IM	TX	130	106	
30	Pictured Rocks National Lakeshore	MW	MI	39	76	
31	Point Reyes National Seashore	PW	CA	88	290	
32	Puukohola Heiau National Historic Site	PW	HI	0.1	2	
33	Redwood National Park	PW	CA	24	58	
34	Salt River Bay National Historic Park & Ecological Preserve	SE	VI	2	2	
35	Sitka National Historic Park	AK	AK	0.2	2	
36	Sleeping Bear Dunes National Lakeshore	MW	MI	42	76	
37	Timucuan Ecological & Historical Preserve	SE	FL	152	2	
38	Virgin Islands Coral Reef National Monument	SE	VI	56	5	
39	Virgin Islands National Park	SE	VI	23	35	25
40	War in the Pacific National Historic Park	PW	GU	4	6	

Appendix 3. Mapping checklist

This list represents a recommended series of steps in an optimal order. Additional steps may be included, and the order of steps may be switched around as long as those changes do not significantly decrease the effectiveness of the mapping process.

- Determine the need. What is the primary reason for mapping?

  - What is the objective of the map (for example, management of oyster reefs)?

  - What area *needs* to be mapped, and why? What areas would be nice to map if possible, and why?

  - What tools and instruments are needed? Can multiple surveys be combined for efficiency?

- Gap analysis. Create a list of missing map information (for example, bathymetry) and a map of where various spatial data exist or are needed.

- Geospatial One-Stop (GOS) announcement. Post information about the planned mapping project.

- Scoping meeting. Hold a meeting to orient key personnel to the mapping plan.

- New data collection. Maximize efficiency and minimize expense by opportunistically combining surveys.

  - Bathymetry

  - Biotic cover

  - Geoform

  - Surficial geology

- Data processing. Retain a copy of the full-resolution raw data for later reprocessing with improved techniques.

- Data interpretation. Initial mapping and classification (draft map).

- Validation of the draft map. Field validation, proxy validation, and expert review.

- Revision of the draft map.

- Expert review and publication. In hard copy and in common digital format.

References

Anderson, T.J., Cochrane, G.R., Roberts, D.A., Chezar, H., and Hatcher, G., 2007, A rapid method to characterize seabed habitats and associated macro-organisms, *in* Todd, B.J., and Greene, H.G., eds., Mapping the seafloor for habitat characterization: Special Paper - Geological Association of Canada, p. 71-79.

Anderson, J.T., Van Holliday, D., Kloser, R., Reid, D.G., and Simard, Y., 2008, Acoustic seabed classification: Current practice and future directions: ICES Journal of Marine Science, v. 65, no. 6, p. 1004-1011.

Andréfouët, S., Hochberg, E.J., Chevillon, C., Muller-Karger, F.E., Brock, J.C., and Hu, C., 2005, Multi-scale remote sensing of coral reefs, *in* Miller, R.L., Del Castillo, C.E., and McKee, B.A., eds., Remote Sensing of Coastal Aquatic Environments: Technologies, techniques and applications: Springer, p. 297-316.

Brock, J.C., Wright, C.W., Clayton, T.D., and Nayegandhi, Amar, 2004, Lidar optical rugosity of coral reefs in Biscayne National Park, Florida: Coral Reefs, v. 23, no. 1, p. 48-59.

Brock, J.C., Wright, C.W., Patterson, Matt, Nayegandhi, Amar, Patterson, Judd, Harris, M.S., and Mosher, Lance, 2006a, EAARL submarine topography: Biscayne National Park: U.S. Geological Survey Open-File Report 2006-1118, accessed at http://pubs.usgs.gov/of/2006/1118/.

Brock, J.C., Wright, C.W., Patterson, Matt, Nayegandhi, Amar, and Travers, L.J., 2007, EAARL topography: Assateague Island National Seashore: U.S. Geological Survey Open-File Report 2007-1176, accessed at http://pubs.usgs.gov/of/2007/1176/.

Brock, J.C., Yates, K.K., Halley, R.B., Kuffner, I.B., Wright, C.W., and Hatcher, B.G., 2006b, Northern Florida reef tract benthic metabolism scaled by remote sensing: Marine Ecology Progress Series, v. 312, p. 123-139.

Brown, C.J., 2007, Seafloor imagery, remote sensing and bathymetry: Acoustic Ground Discrimination Systems (AGDS), *in* Todd, B.J., and Greene, H.G., eds., Mapping the seafloor for habitat characterization: Special Paper - Geological Association of Canada, p. 3-10.

Brown, C.W., Connor, L.N., Lillibridge, J.L., Nalli, N.R., and Legeckis, R.V., 2005, An introduction to satellite sensors, observations and techniques, *in* Miller, R.L., Del Castillo, C.E., and McKee, B.A., eds., remote sensing of coastal aquatic environments: Dordrecht, Netherlands, Springer, p. 21-50.

Casey, K.S., and Cornillon, P., 2001, Global and regional sea surface temperature trends: Journal of Climate, v. 14, no. 18, p. 3801-3818.

Chauvaud, S., Bouchon, C., and Maniere, R., 1998, Remote sensing techniques adapted to high resolution mapping of tropical coastal marine ecosystems (coral reefs, seagrass beds and mangrove): International Journal of Remote Sensing, v. 19, no. 18, p. 3625-3639.

Clausen, C.J., and Arnold, J.B., 1976, The magnetometer and underwater archaeology: Magnetic delineation of individual shipwreck sites, a new control technique: International Journal of Nautical Archaeology, v. 5, no. 2, p. 159-169.

Cochrane, G.R., 2008, Video-supervised classification of sonar data for mapping seafloor habitat, in Reynolds, J.R., and Greene, H.G., eds., Marine habitat mapping technology for Alaska: Fairbanks, Alaska, University of Alaska, p. 185-194.

Cochrane, G.R., Golden, N.E., Dartnell, Pete, Schroeder, D.M., and Finlayson, D.P., 2007, Seafloor mapping and benthic habitat GIS for southern California, Volume III: U.S. Geological Survey Open-File Report 2007-1271, accessed at *http://pubs.usgs.gov/of/2007/1271/*.

Cogan, C.B., and Noji, T.T., 2007, Marine classification, mapping, and biodiversity analysis, in Todd, B.J., and Greene, H.G., eds., Mapping the seafloor for habitat characterization: Special Paper - Geological Association of Canada, p. 129-139.

Collier, J.S., and Humber, S.R., 2007, Time-lapse side-scan sonar imaging of bleached coral reefs: A case study from the Seychelles: Remote Sensing of Environment, v. 108, no. 4, p. 339-356.

Cowardin, L.M., Carter, V., Golet, F.C., and LaRoe, E.T., 1979, Classification of wetlands and deepwater habitats of the United States: U.S. Fish and Wildlife Service FWS/OBS-79/31, 103 p.

Crane, Michael, Clayton, Tonya, Raabe, Ellen, Stoker, Jason, Handley, Larry, Bawden, Gerald, Morgan, Karen, and Queija, Vivian, 2004, Report of the U.S. Geological Survey lidar workshop sponsored by the Land Remote Sensing Program and held in St. Petersburg, FL, November 2002: U.S. Geological Survey Open-File Report 2004-1456, 72 p.

Davis, G.E., 2008, Designing ocean parks for the next century: The George Write Forum, v. 25, no. 3, p. 7-22.

Done, T., and Jones, R., 2006, Tropical coastal ecosystems and climate change prediction: Global and local risks, in Phinney, J.T., Hoegh-Guldberg, O., Kleypas, J., Skirving, W., and Strong, A.E., eds., Coral reefs and climate change: Science and Management: Washington, D.C., American Geophysical Union, p. 5-32.

Gibbs, A.E., Cochran, S.A., Logan, J.B., and Grossman, E.E., 2007, Benthic habitats and offshore geological resources of Kaloko-Honokohau National Historical Park, Hawai`i: U.S. Geological Survey Scientific Investigations Report 2006-5256, p. 62.

Gordon, D.C., McKeown, D.L., Steeves, G., Vass, W.P., Bentham, K., and Chin-Yee, M., 2007, Canadian imaging and sampling technology for studying benthic habitat and biological communities, *in* Todd, B.J., and Greene, H.G., eds., Mapping the seafloor for habitat characterization: Special Paper - Geological Association of Canada 47, p. 29-37.

Gostnell, C., and Yoos, J., 2007, NOAA test and evaluation of interferometric sonar technology: Hydrographic Journal, no. 123, p. 3-8.

Greene, H.G., Bizzarro, J.J., O'Connell, V.M., and Brylinsky, C.K., 2007, Construction of digital potential marine benthic habitat maps using a coded classification scheme and its applications, *in* Todd, B.J., and Greene, H.G., eds., Mapping the seafloor for habitat characterization: Special Paper - Geological Association of Canada, p. 145-159.

Greene, H.G., Wakefield, W.W., Sullivan, D.E., McRea Jr., J.E., Cailliet, G.M., Yoklavich, M.M., Starr, R.M., and O'Connell, V.M., 1999, A classification scheme for deep seafloor habitats: Oceanologica Acta, v. 22, no. 6, p. 663-678.

Hooper, D.U., Chapin, F.S., Ewel, J.J., Hector, A., Inchausti, P., Lavorel, S., Lawton, J.H., Lodge, D.M., Loreau, M., Naeem, S., Schmid, B., Setala, H., Symstad, A.J., Vandermeer, J., and Wardle, D.A., 2005, Effects of biodiversity on ecosystem functioning: A consensus of current knowledge: Ecological Monographs, v. 75, no. 1, p. 3-35.

Hu, C., Muller-Karger, F.E., Vargo, G.A., Neely, M.B., and Johns, E., 2004, Linkages between coastal runoff and the Florida Keys ecosystem: A study of a dark plume event: Geophysical Research Letters, v. 31, no. 15, p. L15307, doi: 15310.11029/12004GL020382.

Hughes Clarke, J.E., Mayer, L.A., and Wells, D.E., 1996, Shallow-water imaging multibeam sonars: A new tool for investigating seafloor processes in the coastal zone and on the continental shelf: Marine Geophysical Researches, v. 18, no. 6, p. 607-629.

Irvin, B.J., Ventura, S.J., and Slater, B.K., 1997, Fuzzy and isodata classification of landform elements from digital terrain data in Pleasant Valley, Wisconsin: Geoderma, v. 77, no. 2-4, p. 137-154.

Jennings, M.D., Faber-Langendoem, D., Loucks, O.L., Peet, R.K., and Roberts, D., 2009, Standards for associations and alliances of the U.S. National Vegetation Classification: Ecological Monographs, v. 79, no. 2, p. 173-199.

Jokiel, P.L., and Brown, E.K., 2004, Global warming, regional trends and inshore environmental conditions influence coral bleaching in Hawaii: Global Change Biology, v. 10, no. 10, p. 1627-1641.

Kendall, M.S., and Miller, T., 2008, The influence of thematic and spatial resolution on maps of a coral reef ecosystem: Marine Geodesy, v. 31, p. 75-102.

LaPointe, B.E., 1997, Nutrient thresholds for bottom-up control of macroalgal blooms on coral reefs in Jamaica and southeast Florida: Limnology and Oceanography, v. 42, p. 1119-1131.

Lidz, B.H., Brock, J.C., and Nagle, D.B., 2008, Utility of shallow-water ATRIS images in defining biogeologic processes and self-similarity in skeletal Scleractinia, Florida reefs: Journal of Coastal Research, v. 24, no. 5, p. 1320-1338.

Lundblad, E.R., Wright, D.J., Miller, J., Larkin, E.M., Rinehart, R., Naar, D.F., Donahue, B.T., Anderson, S.M., and Battista, T., 2006, A benthic terrain classification scheme for American Samoa: Marine Geodesy, v. 29, no. 2, p. 89-111.

Ma, Z., and Redmond, R.L., 1995, Tau coefficients for accuracy assessments of classification of remote sensing data, Photogrammetric Engineering and Remote Sensing, v. 61, no. 4, p. 435.

Madden, C. J., K. Goodin, R.J. Allee, G. Cicchetti, C. Moses, M. Finkbeiner, D. Bamford, 2009, Coastal and Marine Ecological Classification Standard. NOAA and NatureServe. 107 p., accessed at http://www.csc.noaa.gov/benthic/cmecs/CMECS_v3_20090824.pdf.

Madden, C, K. Goodin, B. Allee, M. Finkbeiner, D. Bamford. 2008, Coastal and Marine Ecological Classification Standard. NOAA and NatureServe. 77p., accessed at http://www.natureserve.org/publications/coastalMarineDraft3.pdf.

Madden, C.J., Grossman, D.H., and Goodin, K.L., 2005, Coastal and marine systems of North America: Framework for an ecological classification standard, Version II: NOAA and NatureServe, 40 p.

McIntyre, M.L., Naar, D.F., Carder, K.L., Donahue, B.T., and Mallinson, D.J., 2006, Coastal bathymetry from hyperspectral remote sensing data: Comparisons with high-resolution multibeam bathymetry: Marine Geophysical Researches, v. 27, no. 2, p. 128-136.

Moses, C.S., Andréfouët, S., Kranenburg, C.J., and Muller-Karger, F.E., 2009, Regional estimates of reef carbonate dynamics and productivity using Landsat 7 ETM+, and potential impacts from ocean acidification: Marine Ecology Progress Series, v. 380, p. 103-115.

Moses, C.S., Nayegandhi, Amar, Brock, J.C., and Beavers, Rebecca, 2010, USGS-NPS Servicewide Benthic Mapping Program (SBMP) workshop report: U.S. Geological Survey Open-File Report 2010-1194, 38 p., accessed at http://pubs.usgs.gov/of/2010/1194/.

Mumby, P.J., Green, E.P., Edwards, A.J., and Clark, C.D., 1997, Coral reef habitat-mapping: How much detail can remote sensing provide?: Marine Biology, v. 130, no. 2, p. 193-202.

Myers, J.S., and Miller, R.L., 2005, Optical airborne remote sensing, *in* Miller, R.L., Del Castillo, C.E., and McKee, B.A., eds., Remote Sensing of Coastal Aquatic Environments: Dordrecht, Netherlands, Springer, p. 51-68.

National Park Service, Natural resource inventory and monitoring guidelines (NPS 75), p. 40.

National Park Service, Natural resources management reference manual #77, p.

Nelson, K., and Beavers, R., 2002, Coastal geology mapping protocols for the Atlantic and Gulf National Park units: National Park Service NPS-D-2269, 48 p.

NPS Submerged Cultural Resources Unit, 1998, *H.L. Hunley* site assessment: National Park Service, 198 p.

Poppe, L.J., Paskevich, V.F., Butman, B., Ackerman, S.D., Danforth, W.W., Foster, D.S., and Blackwood, D.S., 2005, Geological interpretation of bathymetric and backscatter imagery of the sea floor off eastern Cape Cod, Massachusetts: U.S. Geological Survey Open-File Report 2005-1048, p. accessed at: *http://woodshole.er.usgs.gov/pubs/of2005-1048/index.htm.*

Prada, M., Appeldoorn, R., and Rivera, J., 2008, The effects of minimum map unit in coral reefs maps generated from high resolution side scan sonar mosaics: Coral Reefs, v. 27, no. 2, p. 297-310.

Quintal, R.T., Dysart, P., and Greene, R., 2007, Automated side-scan data analysis: A system for target detection, classification and measurement: Hydro International, v. 11, no. 9, p. 22-25.

Stumpf, R.P., Holderied, K., and Sinclair, M., 2003, Determination of water depth with high-resolution satellite imagery over variable bottom types: Limnology and Oceanography, v. 48, no. 1, p. 547-556.

U.S. Geological Survey, 1999, Map accuracy standards, U.S. Geological Survey Fact Sheet 171-99, 2 p.

Zawada, D.G., Thompson, P.R., and Butcher, J., 2008, A new towed platform for the unobtrusive surveying of benthic habitats and organisms: Revista de Biologia Tropical, v. 56, no. 1, p. 51-63.